NAPPY JOURNEY

The Twisted Road to Natural Hair

By

Sharon D. Chappelle Ph.D.

ISBN: 1-4033-1299-0 (e-book)
ISBN: 1-4033-1300-8 (Paperback)

This book is printed on acid free paper.

1st Books - rev. 07/31/03

Dedication

I dedicate this book to all those Kinky, Nappy, Knotty, Peazy Nubian headed Queens! Love your crowns of glory they are a source and acknowledgement of strength. They are indeed a GOD given gift!

Peace & Blessings
Sharon

Acknowledgements

It is difficult to put into words how grateful I am for all the gifts GOD has given me. I acknowledge that with out Him I have and am nothing.

I am blessed with a supportive, loving and yes sometimes critical but always caring husband. Fred you often say I inspire you, well, you inspire me! Your quiet way, your gentle nudges (even when I am snoring!) your push to have me meet my goals, fuel me. Thank-you , for your time in editing this book. I love you!

Collin and Corey. Once again you have watched your mother embark on yet another new project. I love the fact that you never question and always support. Thank-you for the times you came into the office after a long day at school to chat, laugh and connect with me. Always know that no matter how busy I get or whatever the next new project may be I love you!

To Kathy your support, love, and caring has meant that I have stood in the possibility of the future and created it! Thank-You.

To all my sister-friends and those who have made this book a reality...truly there would not be a book without your willingness to share. Thank-you for letting others see your laughter and your tears.

To Dori, thank-you for your gift and talent of drawing. Your illustrations speak to the heart.

To all our foremothers, history made it difficult for you to love yourself the way GOD created you. I now know that without that history and your struggle...My Journey would not have existed. Ashay to you. I will never forget!

Contents

Introduction
The Nappy Journey

The Nappy Journey does not have to be painful
It can be fun and full of joy

The curls of your hair lifting up to the heavens kissing
the angels as they pass by.

The Nappy Journey does not have to bring tears
It can be one of rejoicing and full of fun

As the soft rain falls caressing and encouraging each
strand to stand and cheer!

The Nappy Journey does not have to bring shame
It can be a halo of strength and full of fame

Each coil of hair weaving a story of hope and love to
share

So shed no more tears, no ouches or please stop!
The Nappy Journey is a sacred thing
One to rejoice and give thanks for that wave, that bend,
that kink, that nap
Rejoice in God's gift with thanksgiving

Part I
Our Hair-History

Nappy Journey
The Twisted Road to Natural Hair!

There is a history to our hair. In the book "Hair Story: Untangling the Roots of Black Hair in America" by Ayana D. Byrd & Lori Tharps…(a book I read in one day!) that history is made clear.

It seems important to share our collective "Nappy Story" as it relates to our history before going any further. Our hair has been a functional messenger of our culture for centuries. Functional in that the very texture (and there are many) provided a natural barrier to the hot sunny climates of the African Continent. A messenger in that for many tribes and or clans a hairstyle denoted: social class, marital status, religion, age, clan affiliation, geographic region, status within the community, as well as its spiritual significance.

Intricate, braids, twist and styles were beautifully adorned. Adorning of the hair with shells, beads, flowers, cloths and natural dyes such as mud continues to be true in today's Africa as well as throughout the African Diaspora.

During the slave trade, these beautiful ornate hairstyles were not lost on the captors. Although they may have been totally unaware of the specific significance of each style these cunning men immediately knew the importance of the process of dehumanization. What better way to begin that process than to shave each person's head? Thus, the process began of stripping one's status, culture, and ultimately the sense of self and belonging.

The discussion of hair seems trivial when discussing slavery. But it is important to understand slavery's connection to today and the issue of our hair, its perceived beauty or lack there of. My attempt is not to trivialize this period but to assist in making a connection to our past and our hair today.

In 18th century Georgia, North Carolina, Virginia or Alabama there were none of the usual tools used for grooming. No African Combs (similar to today's hair picks), no palm oil or fresh flowers and herbs used for washing and conditioning. The inhumane conditions for working and living left little time to worry about the grooming of hair. **What was once a cultural connection of hours spent in braiding, twisting, adorning and connecting did not exist.**

Hair became matted and often the scalp infested with parasites such as ringworm and/or lice. Makeshift scarves were used to cover up the once beautiful crown of glory.

As time passed an interesting thing occurred, as in Africa but in a different way, it became possible to determine what type of work a slave did by how they wore their hair. The closer a slave was to the white slave owner i.e. working as cooks, seamstresses, carriage drivers, housekeepers and the like; hair tended to be groomed (often using tools used to shear and care for sheep) either in cornrows or braids. By the late 1700's, occasionally women would attempt to emulate their white female slave owners by imitating their hairstyles. Because of the kinky nature of their hair this was very difficult to do. Men could be seen wearing white wigs as their male slave owners did. One wonders if this is one of the first times our ancestors began to receive the message that African hair was **"BAD HAIR"**.

Men who did more of the manual labor tended to shave their heads, while the women covered their heads with scarves. As African's were forced (whether directly or indirectly) into sexual relationships with their white slaver owners; mixed race children were born. Those children with genes from both parents were often with lighter pigment and with straight, wavy or curly hair. We all know how the story goes here!! The closer to white you were the more you were accepted. **So in a world dominated by a white aesthetic of beauty, dark, kinky headed Africans were relegated to being considered ugly.**

Dehumanizing terms were used to portray these individuals considered to be property. At the slave market or on runaway posters, words such as "wooly hair" "skin like the night" and "full monkey lips" were often used. The white beauty ideal had become established. The message was definitely loud and clear… black people particularly women were not pretty!!! A multi-generational message had begun. And thus that message started its historical journey, being passed down in so many verbal and non-verbal ways generation after generation.

Time slowly evolved into new centuries. The Atlantic Slave trade was outlawed; no new Africans were being introduced to the slave population. Without the reminder of cultural pride in ones hair, language and custom that "your hair is not pretty" message developed into an adopted practice of attempting to have African hair look like white hair. A strong desire to straighten one's hair began to manifest itself.

"Without the combs, herbal ointments, and palm oil used in Africa for hairdressing, the slaves were forced to use common Western household products and equipment to achieve certain styles, Instead of palm oil, the slaves took to using oil-based products like bacon grease and butter to condition and soften hair, prepare it for straightening, and make it shine. Cornmeal and kerosene were used as scalp cleaners, and coffee became a natural dye for women"[1]

Ingenuous methods were developed to straighten the hair. A butter knife heated and run across the hair. Warmed cloths were tied over the head. Lye mixed with potatoes was placed on the hair to smooth and straighten.

These methods gave birth to the development of not only a wide spread beauty ideal but to a multimillion dollar business, a business that few Blacks have benefited from but have contributed to in a heft way. Centuries of messages were so internalized!

Our Hair-History is one of pride, pain and eventual payoff. Centuries of messages of being ugly, inferior, or not human unfortunately created a desire to emulate the oppressor. Those desires gave rise to **Annie Turnbo Malone, Madame C.J. Walker, and Sarah Spencer Washington** all whom started companies to develop hair straightening/ care products for Blacks. Early black owned companies like, Rose Chemical and

---

[1] Byrd,Ayana & Tharps, Lori, Hair Story Untangling the Roots of Black Hair in America, New York St martin's Press 2001, pg 17

Kashmir Chemical Companies, and Hair Care-Vim Chemical Company followed suit.

Christina Jenkins invented and patented the hair weave. **George E. Johnson** developed Ultra Wave Culture (eventual became Ultra Sheen) and began his hair care empire. Deluxol developed Crème of Nature.

By the 1960s Johnson products held 80 percent of the market, maintaining that hold for the better part of a decade. In 1971 Johnson products became the first black-owned company on the American Stock Exchange. The growth of Johnson products became competition for Revlon.

In 1975, what appeared to be a conspiracy based on race, the Federal Trade Commission (FTC) forced Johnson Products to place a warning on its Ultra Sheen relaxer label. Johnson Products complied, assuming all companies including Revlon had to do the same since they all used Lye. Unfortunately for Johnson Products, the same requirement was not enforced with Revlon. The damage had been done to Johnson's business and reputation. Revlon used that 2-year period to gain a large piece of the ethnic market.

Eventually, Johnson sued the FTC for unfair treatment and won. As a result of the continued White encroachment in the Black hair care business, ten Black hair care manufactures came together and founded the American Health and Beauty Aids Institute (AHBAI). The institute was developed to be a resource and advocate for Black-owned businesses. George Johnson became the founding Chair. **"The Proud Lady"** logo was developed and launched on black owned products. Consumers could now make an informed decision and not be fooled by the attempt of

White-owned manufactures to lure their business by packaging their products in closely similar ways.

As we entered the 1990's a new day was dawning. Magazines such as <u>Essence,</u> <u>Ebony</u> and <u>Jet</u> began to feature, models and entertainers that were sporting "ethnic pride". Visions of braids, cornrows, head wraps and Kente cloth adornments were everywhere.

The hair care market took notice. The development of braid sheens, sprays, oils, dry shampoos and anti-itch products were jumping off the shelves. Black owned and white owned businesses were developing products to meet this growing market not to be out done by their continued efforts in satisfying the **"gotta straighten my hair market"**

Once again the "gotta have my hair straightened market" gave birth to totally new products and entirely new industries. The Weave took off and so did the demand for human and synthetic straight or mildly curly hair. The World Rio Corporation developed "Rio" an "all natural chemical-free relaxer". (Which destroyed, hair, scalp and emotions, resulting in numerous lawsuits). Long flowing straight hair had become a billion dollar industry.

In the background another movement was coming back with a vengeance, a movement to reclaim our identity, strength and beauty. Natural hair was finding a place in the fabric of African-American life. Not just the Afros or cornrows of the past but something different. Locks or Locs or Dreds or Dreadlocks or Nubian locs whatever the terminology, they were here and here to stay! The Loc-movement is a movement born of pride and spirit. Locked heads are multiplying indicating that our sense of self has made a connection to The Spirit of our ancestors in no other way! It is a strong connection one in which I believe we will <u>all</u> get to. Some easier than others!

Part II

The Universe is full of Nappy Headed, Happy People

There is something about the process of locking that has you seeing locked folks all over the place. Of course you see all kinds of heads but the locked heads stand out. In the process of deciding to write this book I concluded that all of those heads had a story to tell. In this section I will tell some of those stories.

Not all those represented have locked or natural heads.... their stories are crucial to understanding the chronology and stages of the process. I am sure you will see yourself represented. You will smile, cry and laugh out loud. ENJOY!!

What follows is a sort of chronology of a new birth of Being.

A chronology connected to where we have been and where we are going.

The stories are varied; each will represent a connection in the Nappy Hair Chronology. Take pleasure in and learn from these stories!

Sharon's Journey

"MY Journey; Back to Freedom!!"

My own story seems to be a good place to start….

I am soon to be 49 years old!! Wow almost a half a century!! Boy that time went fast. It has taken me the better part of 39 of those years to get BACK TO FREEDOM!

I was born around 6am November 22, 1952. **With a "full head" of hair,** I was told. You know the type of hair that the next thing out of some relative's mouth is "well you know its not going to stay like that!" …"yeah and check those ears too!!!"

"Baby Hair" –soft, roll and curl it on your finger. Obedient hair. Hair that is envied, hair that most black folk pray will stay around. Well, my "Baby Hair" decided it would take flight somewhere around my 2nd birthday. The Baby hair was out and Nappy was in!!

I remember my mother talking about trying to comb and braid my hair as a toddler. It was a chore. Squirming, crying, hands flying (both hers and mine). Finally, like most good mothers she resorted to trying to "tackle that Nappy head while I slept." Imagine laying your little head down for a nap, looking one way when you went to bed and waking up looking totally different! I often wonder if that process scared me or if somehow I was intrigued by the magic of it all!!

By the time I started kindergarten I had gotten used to a certain routine. Every day there was the same routine. "Sharon, go get the comb and hair grease". Mind you it wasn't just any hair grease only Royal

Crown and Dixie Peach would do. I preferred, the Dixie Peach, it smelled like fruit. Or did I just think it smelled like fruit because the word peach was in its name??? Anyway, my mother would pull up a kitchen chair in our small living room; put a pillow on the floor between her legs; point at the pillow with that black comb that had several teeth missing …gesturing for me to sit.

These were special times. We would talk about all kinds of things, School, my friends, her job, who was getting on and off her nerves. Occasionally I would be reminded to keep my head still by a swift "POP" to my scalp and a stern "KEEP STILL!"

There where only a few styles my mother's nimble hands would bestow upon my head. There was the **"quick get it done"** 3 braids ..one to the side and two in the back. Or the **"quick get it done but lets make it special"** 3 braids. One to the side, two in the back with a perfect "rolled bang" in the front,(sometimes she would even add ribbons!!). There was the **"church/special occasion "DO""** a bang with two Braids criss- crossed at the top forming a crown. I liked that one. My mother didn't know how to cornrow or French braid, (Why they call it French braiding when all it is an underhand cornrow I'll never know) so she would do the four-braid illusion of a cornrow by parting the hair in four equal sections. Two at the top one either side of my head and connect the top and bottom of each side. Occasionally, she would put a barrette at the end. When she did that I could swing my hair from sided to side. …like the white girls! This was the extent of my Hair-Do's until I was ten years old.

Ten!! Not only had I reached "the 2-numbers" but I could now get my hair straightened. YES!!!! I was excited. Finally, "Straightened Hair"- moving, flowing, straight desirable long hair!! I had no idea what I was getting myself in to. First, let me say my mother was not the best hair straightener. I remember watching her as she did her "touch-up around the edges". Touch-ups occurred in between her standing hairdresser appointment. ... I'll get back to those.... She would turn on the gas-stove, lower the flame and place that heavy cast iron comb on the stove. Heating it..."just a little", she would then take a little bit of hair grease and rub between her palms, smoothing it around her edges. By now the comb was "warm enough". Taking the comb off the burner, blowing on it and rubbing it between the folds of the old towel she would keep handy (I never saw that thing get washed!) ...she would then stand in front of the bathroom mirror and proceed to "Touch-It-Up".....I could see the smoke and smell the "frying" of her hair. And then I heard, "%$^!!!! ,I burned myself! ...Quick Sharon go get me some butter". Butter, the healer of all burns. I think it was suppose to help heal and possibly take care of scarring. So...there she would stand rubbing the butter on the already deeply reddening spot...finishing her "Touch-up".

My turn! Feeling, excited, scared, concerned but wanting to be "beautiful" I was ready. Now understand that straightening or pressing "Virgin Hair" was different than a touch-up.

The process went something like this: First your "Head had to be washed" Halo shampoo was what we used, later would come Prell. Halo, Heavenly Halo.

Your hair was suppose to be like the white-female model on the black and white TV screen after you had used this product. Long, flowing, moving in a heavenly veil of clean BLOND?? Hair. Okay so my hair wouldn't be blond (my actual color when I was young was a "light, reddish, blondish brown" A "Sandy color" my mom would say. Later she said it turned to a Chestnut brown. I think that was from the straightening or maybe later…. the permming…or who knows, maybe it turned colors naturally.

My mother would pull-up a kitchen chair to the sink for me to kneel on as she washed my hair… Everything would be lined up. The Halo shampoo, a towel or two, the black comb with the missing teeth, that pink brush with the incredibly hard bristles, the "Dixie Peach", some wave clamps, a few rubber bands, the strengthening comb and its accompanying "wipe towel". With all the tools of the trade in place she was ready to do battle!

"Is the water too hot?" she would ask as I bent over the running faucet. A muffled "no" would usually be my response. 'What"….I can't hear you", she would often say. I'd try again lifting my face which was being held by my hands…hands that held a towel totally covering my face so that I wouldn't get the "Soap" from the shampoo in my eyes). It's a wonder I didn't suffocate!! I held that thing so tight across my face. NO! I'd yell….**"girl don't raise your voice at me!** …bend over" And the process would begin anew.

The water felt good running over my head. I remember that my 'Virgin-Hair' resisted the water. It took a while before I felt the water reach my scalp. But when it did…ah, Nirvana! "Look at those waves,

Umm…. too bad it won't stay that way" My mother would say. I was thinking what waves??? I had waves! …you mean like the "good hair my cousins had". Why won't they stay"…Oh yeah!! I forgot I had Nappy Hair…not that good Grade –A hair my cousins had. Oh well!!! Let's get back to the process.

After six washings or so - It took that long to get all the **"Dixie Peach"** out of my head from the previous month- my hair would be rinsed several times, each time the water would be a little cooler. "Squeaky-Clean" was what my mother was aiming for. (And it did squeak too) she would ring her hands around my head, pulling the scalp so tight I looked like I was Chinese and I'd hear the squeak. Yep, I was ready for the combing-out process. **Combing-Out- the process by which the once wavy looking, good hair is combed free of its NAPS!**

With my head wrapped in an old towel, we would relocate to the living room and I would once again sit between my mother's legs. The birth of a new "DO" was about to begin, off would come the towel and there was my newly washed and seriously transformed, Halo washed, Nappy hair that looked like the biggest afro you'd ever seen. (It was a vision of things to come.)

Teeny section by section my mother would comb out the naps, snarls and kinks! She would try hard not to hurt me by holding the section of hair close to my scalp and using quick, short strokes she would comb it out. I hated this part. When I would yell ouch…which was often, her response was "That didn't hurt…so sit still". What is it about parents who always tell you what hurts and doesn't hurt? I wanted to say back "Its not your head, so don't' tell me it doesn't hurt." Of course I never did! Talking back was a "federal offense!!! Punishable by a serious whopping!.. So I would endure! Section by section she would repeat this process twisting each section, wrapping it around itself to form a knot. (Later, I discovered that these would be called "Nubian Knots") My head was completely combed out in about an hour. And we still were not done!

We would relocate once again…back to the kitchen. The burner would be lit, the straightening comb put in place to get HOT NOT WARM. Virgin Nappy Hair required a HOT comb!!! Why a Hot comb I wondered as my mother loosened one of my knots…my hair already looked pretty straight to me!

"Now Sharon, you have to sit still". I watched, as she would place glob of Dixie Peach on the back of her left hand. She would take small amounts; put some on my scalp and some on the strands of almost straight hair. Next she would remove the comb from the burner and begin to "Press" my hair…blowing as she pulled through my already, almost straight hair. Was my hair on FIRE????!!! There was so much smoke and that hissing sound…what was that?…**just keep still I told my self and it won't hurt!**

Section by section my Afro was transformed into this long, silky, thin, flat lifeless stuff. This was not the flowing, silky, bouncing stuff I saw on TV…. Another forty-five minutes or so had gone by and I wasn't done yet! "Mom…what about my curls?" No curls for me she would explain. "I'll section off a bang and put a roller in it…the rest we'll put into a "Pig-Tail". Now a "Pig-Tail" is different that a Pony-Tail and neither is what I had in mind. Pigtails were the double twist, barrette on the end version of the pony-tail…. definitely not what I had in mind. But of course, I better not "Talk-Back". So, there I sat as my mother brushed my already tender scalp (different than Tender-Headed…I was not tender-headed…if I was I would have surely already died from the battle!!)…pull it all together place a rubber band around it and made my Pig-tail. She then proceeded to spritz a little water on the flat lifeless section of hair that was to be my bang. WATER??? Why was she doing that? Did we not just spend close to two and a half hours on getting rid of what water naturally does to my head??? I don't get it. "Oh, the water will give it a little body so your bang will curl." You mean I could have had curls all over my head if it wasn't pressed…this was truly confusing! The now washed, pressed, greased and now water spritzed section would be rolled into a medium, pink hard roller…to form my bang. In just another half-hour I would have a completed, pressed Do! I couldn't wait for my bang to form. **THREE HOURS LATER I WAS READY!!!!** Maybe it would be easier to be bald!!!!

What a process!!! Pressing allowed me to have increasing number of "Do's". In addition to the pig-tail/bang, there was the Bun with tendrils. Not the type of old-lady bun at the back of your head but the bun at the top of your head. Tendrils, were the Shirley Temple looking curls that were strategically placed around your heard. They gave the appearance of wisps of good hair. All of these styles were reserved for SUNDAY. There was no way there was time to go through this process during the school week.

Sometimes my mother would try and preserve the Sunday style by tying my head up at might with one of her rayon kerchiefs. (They weren't called "scarfs" and they were definitely not silk) This worked well only for a day or so. By Tuesday the Naps were back! And I was back to braids. Funny I hated braids then and grew to love them fifteen years later.

The first time I was allowed to have my hair 'loose" was when I was ten and a half. Easter was coming and I begged to have "Shirley Temple Curls". I wanted curls just like the little white girl I saw dancing with Mr. Bojangles. Oh, how those curls bounced as they danced up and down those stairs. The begging paid off. I got my very first hairdresser appointment.

My mother had a bi-weekly standing appointment at a little storefront beauty shop near Front Street, right across the street from the Shop-Rite. She had been going to the same place for years.

Miss Picket owned the shop and she was my mother's hairdresser. There were two other beauticians, Mary and Ruth, who also did hair, but not my mother's …no, it was Miss Picket or nobody!

Walking in the door of the hairdresser, all of your senses were invaded. The sounds, sights and smells were over powering. People were talking, phones ring, dryers going, the clicking of the hot curlers, the sound of water running, scissors clipping and razors shaping and of course the occasional "hey Girl, were you been". You could smell the hair frying, shampoos, conditioners, and chicken and fish sandwiches from the store around the corner, cigarettes, and something that smelled like rotten eggs. …. (I would later find out that the rotten egg smell was from the chemicals in the perms.)

There were always women waiting in the tiny sitting area to the left of the doorway. The **"kitchen chairs"** that were now transformed to **waiting –room chairs** were always filled. Usually there were one or two people sitting in the 'window"…it really wasn't a window-seat it was a recessed window that served as a stand for old, Ebony's, Jets,, The Mohammad Speaks, hair-books and at times a Family Circle or a Readers Digest. The reading material was never current. There were magazines there with no covers that were at least three years old!!! But when you are waiting, sometimes for an hour or two for an appointment you thought you had an hour or two ago, the magazines kept you busy. That is if you weren't joining in on the conversation about whatever gossip was going around at the time.

The Saturday before Easter is the busiest day of the year in a Black- Hair salon! That's still the case today. Everyone wants their new "DO" to be as fresh as possible for the Sunrise Service, the Breakfast after and the Easter Sunday Worship Service after that. So you prepare yourself to wait, and wait some more.

One Saturday morning before Easter in 1963 I waited my turn; entertained by the happenings in Miss Picket's Beauty shop. When my turn came, Miss Picket called my name. "Sharon, Ok Baby lets go". As I walked the gauntlet of people, sounds and smells, my mother gave Miss Picket instructions. I sat in the chair and my mother looked at me and said she would be back later. She was leaving me!

Miss Picket undid my braids and brushed my hair back. Then she put a small towel around my neck and a vinyl cape around me. She lowered the chair and had me follow her to the back of the salon. I walked pass Miss Mary and Miss Ruth and several customers under the dryer. I noticed that the once yellow walls weren't really yellow but a dingy, kind of yellow with stains on them.

The back of the salon had two hair washing sinks. One was black and the other was pink. I sat on some pillows at the black one leaned my head back, as she ran warm water over my head.

The shampoo smelled wonderful! It definitely wasn't Halo or Prell. Once shampooed, she placed a conditioner on my hair with a plastic cap, and I sat under the dryer for what seemed like an hour. I am sure it wasn't. The conditioner was rinsed out and I went back to Miss Picket's chair to have my hair blow-dried. Section by section she simultaneously pulled the comb and dryer through my hair. Wow, my hair looked great! Almost like a long, puffed out Afro. As she moved the chair around to reach other sections, my hair would blow toward my face. It felt so soft and smelled a little like cotton candy. Maybe, we should just leave it like this, I thought. Yeah I like it like this. So, I said to Miss Picket…"I like this style… lets leave it!" I still can remember her face when she looked at me and said "Baby, no way this ain't no style; your mother would kill me if I let you walk out of here with your hair all over your head like this!" So she proceeded to press my hair. I could here the sizzling. And as I took glimpses of myself in the mirror I saw the life leave my hair. It was no longer, alive and vibrant. It was not hair you noticed - it was flat! And it didn't move!

Making the Shirley Temple curls was the next stage. Miss Picket put her medium sized curling iron on the small burner that looked like it had teeth. She smeared the back of her left hand with an orange curling wax. Placing small amounts on the separated strands she formed my Shirley Temple curls. Now, as I snatched glimpses of myself in the mirror I watched the miracle of the development of a head full of curls. My hair had come back to life!!! I even had a part on the side of my head. Just like Shirley Temple had as she danced down the steps with Mr. Bojangles. The rite of passage of my first hairdresser appointment was completed. I was ready for Easter Sunday!

That night, my mother carefully tied my head up. I remember trying to prop my pillow up so I could sleep sitting up. That way I knew I would not spoil my – "DO! Easter Sunday morning 1963 I was ready. My curls had survived the night. Dressed and ready to go out the door my mother told me I had forgotten something. What could it be, I thought. I had on my new "White" dress. It actually was a First Communion dresses I saw at the Newark "Alexander" store. I had my gloves and shoes, what could she be talking about? "Your Hat...get your hat and lets go". No way was I going to mess up my bouncing, shiny new Shirley Temple "DO" with a hat. I said, "but I don't want to wear the hat any more!" Why did I say that!. My mother went into her usual litany about my being ungrateful, the money she had spent etcetera, etcetera. And if I didn't put that hat on she was going to beat my behind. Needless to say I put the white straw hat on my head. I was not happy! Smash went my Shirley Temple Curls, no more white girl bouncing hair for me.

I did not get my hair done often by Miss Picket, only once a year, the Saturday before Easter.

The sixty's were an interesting time. Civil rights, the assassinations of President Kennedy, Dr. King, Malcolm X and Medgar Evers, impacted all our lives. Demonstrations against the Vietnam War, the massacre at Kent State University and other now historical events were daily news occurrences, back then. It was also the birth of the "Black is Beautiful Movement". All of a sudden…or it seemed that way. The term Negro was out and Black was in style. Black was no longer a word that started fistfights. It was a word used to ignite a sense of pride and belonging. I remember singing along when radio station WBLS played James Brown's "I am Black and I am Proud" released in 1969. "Say it Loud…I am Black and I am proud", I'd sing as I danced around the house in my new "DO"…**THE AFRO, FRO ,BUSH or NATURAL.** I called mine an Afro.

I was a teenager during this time and having an Afro was a necessary part of my rebellion. My mother wasn't all that thrilled about **this** new "DO".

Now, it is important to note that I did not wear my Afro on a daily basis. It was too much work for me to get my hair to look like that of Angela Davis, my new hair-role-model. YEP! A black female "hair-ro"! (My attempt at humor – get it? Hero – hair-ro) My hair just did not want to get Nappy enough!!! So, I would resort to washing it, putting a small amount of **"Dippity-Do /Dixie Peach"** mix on each section; making small braids and rolling those small braids on pieces of

27

brown paper bag. (I didn't want the pink sponge rollers to pull my hair out…besides it took too much time to put those end papers on to try and prevent that very thing from happening. The paper-bag would be just fine. I would usually have to wait hours for my hair to dry. Then, I would take out my brown paper bag rollers, unbraid each prequel to the Nubian knot, fluff with my fingers and finally get my new red, black and green **"Freedom Pick"** and pick out my Afro. With a little pat here and there to make sure it was the desired shape and you couldn't see through it I was ready! I envisioned myself as Angela Davis. I was aware of "The Struggle", wore my homemade Dashiki and I was a quasi-politician (Secretary of my Junior class). Occasionally, I would leave my braids in and wrap my head up in a **Gelee'** (African head-wrap) feeling like a proud African-Queen.

But that changed just prior to my sixteenth birthday. It was at that point that I wanted desperately to have my hair cut. A hair cut also meant I would need a perm. **WHAT WAS I THINKING!!**

Now getting your hair cut is a big deal for most black families. It starts when we are babies. You'll never see a black family cut a little boy's hair until his first maybe even his second birthday! For girls its sacrilegious to even think about it. Or lets put it this way, - If you are blessed with a Nappy head of hair like mine was, you at least want it to be long. That way there is something to "admire". The myth was and still is - **NAPPY HAIR DOES NOT GROW.** The ironic thing is, if it has grown thus far, why would cutting it stop it from growing??

So when I announced to my mother I wanted a hair cut everybody got involved. My great-grandmother, great-aunt, my mother's friends; Fredda-Mae and Martha. I am not sure what concerned them the most; the fact that I was no longer going to look like the militant Afro wearing, Angela-Davis wanna-be. Or that that I wanted to cut my hair! Thank GOD for Martha. With her intervention, my mother agreed.

Once again Miss Picket held another rite of passage in her hands. My first Perm was a "Vigrol". This "Vigrol" was yellow and came in a clear bottle. The smell was worse then rotten eggs. Miss Picket assured me that it had less lye… (LYE! Wasn't that the stuff that could burn holes through metal?), so it wouldn't do as much damage. I really don't think I understood the implications of "as much damage"!! Now I do!!!

My hair was washed, conditioned, permed and cut. The cut almost looked like Twiggy's . You know, Twiggy the skinny white model from England. (Do you notice my desire to have my hair look like white girls once again!) I was quite taken with my new look! Of course, the feedback was, **YOUR HAIR WILL NEVER GROW BACK!** For the moment I didn't care. I had a new" Do", a new dress, new shoes and a sweet sixteen party my mother gave me at The Shady Rest Country Club in Scotch Plains, New Jersey.

Well, my hair did grow back!

Of course the nay Sayers indicated it still wasn't like it use to be. I figured I always had "thin hair" so there was no problem as far as I was concerned. I continued to have my perm retouched at the prescribed intervals. By my senior year I had enough hair to

29

purchase a fall. I decided it was taking to long to grow back so why not add a little to the back of my head! I purchased the fall from a small wig shop that had opened on Third near Plainfield Avenue. That place was a Godsend. I decided on a fall of synthetic hair with absolutely gorgeous Shirley Temple curls! My "updated" Shirley Temple look was so great (so I thought) that I decided to wear it for my high school graduation pictures. When people see this picture I am often asked, **"Is that your hair?"** My response was always a curt **"I bought it didn't I!!"**

In retrospect, I know I was embarrassed, ashamed and to a degree disappointed with my need to attach some fake hair to my head. Although my concerns and feelings about this need were strong, they were not strong enough to interfere with my ongoing use of attachments, and wigs.

Through –out college I had numerous, wigs, falls, braids, ponytails and afro-puffs. I would often hunt for wig stores, comparing their product to what I was currently using. Should I change the color, what about something a little "nappier'….it might look more authentic. Occasionally, I would tire of these hairpieces and I would cut my hair into a sought after style…of course I was continuing to perm my hair. By now I had graduated to the use of the 'Ultra Sheen" perm in the mild formula. (Surely I was doing no damage to my hair by using a mild perm!!)

In the early to mid 70's Braids made a come back. Not the braids I use to despise when I was younger, new more sophisticated style became the rage. Many actresses, politicians and noteworthy individuals began sporting intricate cornrow styles; as well as "extension" braids. The reflection of The Motherland could be seen all over America.

In 1975 I graduated undergraduate school, by then I was addicted to having my hair braided with extensions. I preferred "human-hair" vs. synthetic- it behaved better. I could roll it, curl it wash it with no problems.

Being addicted to having your hair braided with extensions comes with a price. That price includes:

- Finding someone who knows how to braid
- Sitting for 6 to 8 hours to have it braided
- Unbraiding it (which usually took double the amount of time it took to braid it)
- Washing, conditioning and combing your now unbraided "natural hair" in preparation to start the process all over again!

I would be remiss if I just mentioned the cost of such a "DO". Lets look at the benefits:

- Long, manageable hair
- Increased styling options
- "Get-up & go" hair
- No fuss no muss for about 3months
- Change your hair color on a whim
- And of course it looked good!

During this period Valencia, my college buddy located a wonderful braider. A Black woman with a French accent!! Her name was Amnique . She lived in Paris most of her life after her family emigrated from the French speaking Caribbean. Amnique was indeed the braider de jour! She lived in this wonderful artsy loft in Norwalk, Connecticut. The kind of place that makes you feel grown-up and cool. Often jazz would be playing in the background as she bestowed upon your head this masterful style…. the ambiance itself made you feel special!

Eventually, cost became a factor. Motivated by the challenge and the cost Valencia started paying very close attention to the extension process. It did not take long before she had mastered the braiding process. Not only was she able to braid others she could do her own. YES! I was ecstatic. Valencia became my braider of choice. Not only could she braid her you know what off!! She also didn't charge me a fortune.

So every 2 to 3 months I would make the trip to her apartment and she would braid my hair. Soon, Valencia began to convince me that I to could learn how to do my own hair. I was a little Skeptical, but after a few lessons I got the hang of it.

I figured in the years that I braided my own hair I had saved a fortune. Braiding my own hair was a snap. I had gotten it down to a science. After I washed, conditioned and blew-dry my hair I would set up shop!

I needed lots of "tools"…..

- 4 bags of human hair number, two #2s & two #4s
- A "rat-tail" comb
- The jar of Blue-Magic hair grease
- A couple of clips and or rubber bands
- A mirror
- 3 chairs, one to sit in with pillows, one to prop the mirror in front of me, and one to hold the hair and other utensils

Once I was all set up, I braided until I was finished. Initially it took me about 6 hours to complete but within 6months I was down to four. Not only had I reduced my cost, I reduced my sitting time by 50%! Unfortunately for some reason I couldn't do other peoples' hair. I tried but the extension just wouldn't hold! No one wants to walk around and find a braid lying round. So I didn't make money out of my newfound skill. Oh well!!! You can't have everything.

I had my hair in extensions from around 1975 to the early 80's. I can pinpoint a change in my perception of myself, including my hair, to getting pregnant with my first child.

Many questions would come to me regarding this major change in my life. My husband would often look at me like I had lost my mind when I would say to him…"Honey I don't think mothers wear blue cowboy boots" (I was completely serious…I had a pair of blue cowboy boots that I loved…and yes they were in style…I actually bought them in NYC!). Or I might ask numerous questions about, how I should look act and behave.

I took my braids out shortly after my son was born and got a radical haircut. I have no idea why but I did. **A friend suggested I try a salon near our house. I was a little concerned. No...the word is worried because it was a "white salon".** She assured me it would be fine. "Just look at my hair " she said.

Yes, it was true her haircut was great, so I decided why not; my hair would grow back…wouldn't it???

The stylist (not hairdresser) was a white male who volunteered he was Gay. Now I wouldn't make note of this fact, except for the stereotype of Gay men had been drummed into me since I was young. They were great decorators, dressed impeccably, were great choir directors and wonderful hair stylists. So, based on the stereotype (I have since broadened my idea about Gays) I knew I was in good hands.

I had no idea what type of cut I wanted. I just knew I wanted something cool and easy to care for. Gary insisted he knew just the look for me. "Do you trust me?' he said. My reply was a weak, yes. I am sure he did not pick up on the weakness of the response. As he proceeded I reminded him I did not want it to be too short. "No problem it wouldn't be", he assured me. He washed and permed, conditioned and blew dry my hair. Wow, my hair had grown. It was well pass my shoulders. I hadn't seen its "true length" (whatever that is) in about seven years. Who said black hair doesn't' grow. As I looked at how long it was I had second thoughts. Maybe I should just leave it alone. Look how long it was! A few curls and I would have bouncing and behaving hair. As I savored that image, I could hear a voice in the background. **"Sharon are you ready?"** Jolted back to reality!! Right…. I am here to get my haircut!

As Gary prepared to cut, he made me promise not to look in the mirror until he was done. I made my pact not to look and started praying silently.

That buzzing sound …what was that? Before I could even finish the thought, I felt Gary's left hand on top of my head, slightly nudging me to move my head forward. "What? What? What is he doing?" Surely he is not going to give me a buzz cut!!! Oh GOD, help me! He must have sensed my concern and reassured me I wouldn't be bald. Dutifully, I followed the pressure of his hand and put my head down.

I could feel the vibrations of the clippers before they touch my scalp. Hmmm…they are not touching my scalp, I thought…this is good…it'll be fine. The clipping didn't take long. When he stopped I was sure he would move to the top of my head. But, he didn't. He pulled out those little sharp scissors and started cutting. I could see little snips of hair falling in front of my face. I was still thinking this is going to work. Finally, he moved to the top of my head. I could hear the scissors snipping away. Finally, he stopped. Was he done? Nope!! He wasn't. Gary explained that he was going to use a razor for shaping. WHAT??? A razor. Now I must admit my first thought was "this white guy must be crazy!" Once again he assured me not to worry. "You are going to love this cut".

Two hours from start to finish, Gary twirled me around so that I was facing the mirror. While moving I took a peak at the floor and saw what must have been a bushel of hair on the floor. **OH MY GOD!** In a flash I was facing the mirror looking at my reflection. Relief!!! It looked ok. It would take some getting used to the fact that it seemed to be defying gravity, standing up like that. I figured there was enough hair up there that surely I could comb it down. Make it a little more sedate …mother-like. 'You like?", he said questioningly. Now take a look at the back" Gary said with pride as he handed me the mirror. I gasped and quickly re-grouped. "What do you think?" I could hear him in the background saying. I knew my eyes were welling and I tried to calm my voice so it would not betray my pain. Till this day I can't remember exactly what I said. I do know it was something like…"Oh its shorter than I thought it would be…but it'll grow back"

I made it out of the salon without crying. I approached my car and the tears flowed. As I opened the car door, I sobbed. There I sat in the car trying to calm myself. Trying to convince myself it was okay. I had a haircut that stood –up at the back of my head in such a way that it would not lay down. What was I going to do? Should I stop and by a wig? I decided that was not the answer. I spent the rest of the drive home thinking about my husband's reaction. I walked in the door looked at Fred and started to cry. That night he consoled, supported and laughed with me about my "punk-rock" haircut. It took months before the back of my head grew in to a point where it would lay down. Never once did Fred say a negative word about my hair. Years later he would reveal how much he disliked it.

I maintained a perm for the next thirteen years! I had various styles through this period. I would let it grow and pull it back in a matronly bun. My mother always said I looked good with my hair "off my face". I had it curled in a "page-boy" with a part in the middle of my head. I cut and "wrapped" it for straightness and body!.

Actually, let me take a moment and talk about the "wrapping" process. Wrapping required a definite skill. When I first learned of this technique I was thrilled at the prospect of having my hair be "bone" straight. No ridges at the root. I was even more thrilled at the idea of swingin and movin hair. (Yep…..you got it…back to the white-girl movin hair thang!)

Sherry was my beautician of choice at that time. She was a good friend's sister and she was Black. No more white folks messin in my hair...no way!!!. Sherry had her own shop in New Haven, located in the hood. It wasn't that far from Yale, but far enough that you knew you were not in the Ivy-League section of town. The neighborhood often reminded me of the one where I grew up in New Jersey. There was a mix of two and three family houses, a few small storefronts and very little parking. The shop was a definite throwback to Miss Pickets. It was like being transported back in time. Many of the same sights, smells, sounds and magazines transported me back in time.

It was a tiny shop, three hair stations, a small waiting area in the front and an even smaller washing area in the back. You could even buy some fried chicken or meat patties across the street at the small deli own by a Latino family.

On one of my "touch-up" visits I asked Sherry about the **swinging-N-behaving** hair I'd seen on lots of sisters. She explained the wrapping process. First of course a touch-up was necessary, once the hair was shampooed a large amount of wrapping lotion was applied to the hair. (Sherry used a product called, "Wrap and Tap") after which, she combed my hair using a swirling motion around my head (which was now used as a huge roller). There was so much lotion that I need a towel to hold in front of my face as Sherry comb each strand around my head. When she was finished it looked as if I had a skullcap made of hair on my head. Sherry placed a "Do-Rag" on my head to hold the wrap together. I sat under the dryer for what seemed like 4hours!! It was actually an hour plus a few minutes. I didn't understand why I had to sit there with my head burning up and my ears feeling like they were frying, for so long. I was informed as Sherry checked every 10minutes or so that my hair was the type that holds moisture and moisture was not a good thing if you wanted **swing – N- behaving** hair. So I endured!

It was a relief to finally get from under the dryer. I couldn't wait to see the finished product. Of course I was skeptical about how my big, round, apple-head could be used as a roller and produce the desired results. As, I walked back to the styling chair I peaked in the mirror at my reflection. It revealed nothing. So I slowly moved my hand to my head to touch. My hair felt like straw!! It was stiff and hard. I had a momentary panic. Surely when she started to comb my hair it was all going to comb out!!. I sat in the chair and Sherry used both her hands in a massaging motion "loosing-up my hair". Then a section at a time she started to comb it out. Little by little straight, bouncing, behaving and soft hair appeared! It was a miracle!!! I was amazed at the results.

I left the salon that first day of my first wrap with my hair moving in the Autumn breeze, assured that I would never do anything but a wrap. Over time I perfected the method myself. Purchasing Perm kits, Wrap-N-Tap lotion, a hood dryer and a **"Do-Rag"**. I was in business! No more $35 every two weeks or long waits for my scheduled appointment.

Everyone has a truly close <u>sista-friend</u>. I do, and her name is Kathy. We are so close we are sure somehow we really are sisters. Well Kathy has often been the trend sitter for hair in our relationship. When she got a new "<u>DO</u>", I often followed. So it seemed logical to cut my hair in an almost "Halley Berry Cut" in 1995 after Kathy had gotten hers cut. Monique (Sherry's daughter) provided me with my new look. It was great. I loved it! There was little to no maintenance. (That's because there was little to no hair!) Once I had gotten the cut, I could maintain the style on my own using my wrap method. Every month or so, I would get a shape-up from Monique.

I was content with my haircut for about two years. In 1997 Kathy announced, "I think I am going to let my hair and perm grow-out, and then put braid extensions in". Now, in all honesty, I am not sure if I had an independent thought about the same thing but I decided I would follow suit. My only difficulty was that Kathy made this announcement right after I had gotten my shape-up and trim. So it was going to take me a bit longer to gain enough length to be able to add extensions to my hair. It was even going to take longer for it to grow to a length that I could once again braid my own hair. I was excited and willing to wait.

The search for a new hair braider was on. Kathy was ready to have her hair braided at least a month before I had enough growth. She tried someone locally… it looked good but after a few days the braids started to fall out!! This was indeed a problem. Valencia was living too far away but agreed if Kathy were really stuck she would braid her hair the next time.

Our mutual hunt led us to a Jean. Jean and her mother attended church with Kathy's husband. While at a church sponsored event, Kathy corner Jean to ask where she and her mother got their hair done. To

Kathy's amazement, Jean said she knew of two women who braided hair in Harlem.

Well, we <u>had</u> entertained the thought of going to Harlem or Brooklyn to locate braiders. I had even visited a couple of braiding salons in the Financial District of NYC while on a lunch break from my consulting work, one afternoon. The first seemed dirty, disorganized and unfriendly. The second was way too pricey.

Jean explained to Kathy that we didn't have to go to Harlem. The women came to Middletown on a routine basis!!

Unbelievable!! We could get our hair braided by two sisters from the motherland right in our own hometown. You can't get any better than that!! Sign us up!!!

Our enthusiasm waned a little when we heard the price… $125 a head. Whoa!! That was just about double what we had spent in the past. We conferred and decided it was worth it….just look at Jean and her mom's "<u>DO</u>". How could we not agree to go for it!! So we scheduled a time.

That Saturday couldn't come fast enough. I was finally going to get my hair braided after years of missing the ease of having that style. Kathy was looking forward to having braids that didn't fall out!!

We arrived at the space Jean had rented for this purpose about 15 minutes earlier than scheduled. (She provided transportation for the braiders from Harlem to Connecticut and the space for a cut on each head!! Not a bad arrangement). The Braiding room …Office…space…whatever you want to call it was located above a Polish deli in Middletown. It was raining outside so we stepped into the adjoining door way and waited, and waited and waited. We tried not to doom and gloom; but after 45 minutes had passed we started to panic and get pissed all in the same time period. Kathy decided to give Jean's mother a call. She informed us that Jean had just left to go pick the ladies up at the train station in New Haven.

We knew we were in trouble. New Haven is at least a 35 to 40 minute drive from Middletown. That meant we were looking at waiting at least an hour to an hour and a half before they got to the braiding location. What should we do? Go braid-less, or wait? Now for me, going braid-less meant being "Nappy" and looking tacky!! Neither was a thrilling prospect. So we waited some more…had a great deli sandwich and commiserated about our current predicament. And what a predicament!!

Kathy anticipated that she would be getting her hair braided with hours of spare time before having to attend an evening wedding!!! Big mistake!! I on the other hand had no time constraints. But I was still pissed off!

As we discussed the current situation another women appeared at our doorway waiting area, asking where Jean was. Kathy and I gave each other knowing looks which said "girl you have got to be kidding…she can't be thinking she is going to get her hair done before us…oh no she isn't". I can't remember which one of us responded first. But we let her know that we were now at least 2 hours behind schedule.

So the three of us waited another 20 minutes before the entourage arrived! Jean stepped out of the car apologizing. The two women from the Ivory Coast looked unconcerned while they spoke to each other in French. As we ascended the stairs, Jean told the new arriver that her appointment would have to be moved about 4hours. Amazingly she did not appear to be to upset. Hmmm, maybe this meant that being late was to be expected. Well, we would be prepared for the next time, I thought.

Lare' and Maxine, our imported braiders got themselves ready. Jean turned the radio on and went to put on a pot of coffee as she apologized again about the late start. Lare' and Maxine had missed the first train and had to wait an hour for the next one. As Lare' called Kathy over to the chair the door open and in walked a mother and her teenage daughter.

Jean looked surprised and then with recognition. After a glance at her watch walked over to them, explained that there had been not only a missed train but also a mix up in their appointment time.

The mother and the daughter departed.... they were not happy campers!! I sat in silence flipping through several photo albums of styles the ladies had bestowed upon other customers as I observed the latest interaction! I was waiting patiently for my turn.

Finally it was time. Maxine motioned to me as she spoke to her sister in French. For all I know she could have been calling me some name. I am not sure if it was just the fact that they choose not to speak in English, or was it their serious, unfriendly behavior that ignited my prejudice. I found myself feeling somewhat uncomfortable and annoyed.

I shared with Maxine my desire to have individual small extensions throughout my head. She nodded in understanding and proceeded to braid. Occasionally

Kathy and I would talk but mainly we sat next to one another silently flipping through an old Ebony or Jet magazine.

Four hours later Kathy was finished. Her hair looked wonderful. She said her goodbyes and off to the wedding she went. An hour or so later Maxine was finished with my hair. I was pleased!! Actually, more than pleased I was delighted. **My new swinging braided "Do" was- da BOMB!!.** I even had highlights braided in.

I paid my $125, no tip added. I still had an attitude about what I perceived to be their attitude. Later as I look back, I feel somewhat childish about this response. But you can't go back to things that have passed and change your response.

Our new braided styles lasted over three months. Typically, three months is the limit for leaving extensions in your hair. But, these extensions were so finely done that there was no fuzzing, frizzing or fussing required. The new growth wasn't as visible and it gave me unlimited style possibilities. I wore it curled, pony tailed, French rolled and corn rowed. Every possible braid style imaginable, I tried. I remember that Amnik once said that braids could do anything. She was right.

Well we finally did get to the point of needing to have our hair redone. This was a dilemma. What to do? Spend another $125 or look for someone new. We decided on the latter. We were on the hunt! Kathy would check her resources and I would check mine.

I found a new braider by making several phone calls to friends. Her name was Maria. Maria lived in Hartford in this wonderful old home not far from the

Governor's mansion. She was of Caribbean descent by way of England. She had a wonderful British accent and a warm friendly personality.

I was the first to try her as a braider and made an appointment for a Saturday morning. I arrived at 7:45am, fifteen minutes before our agreed upon time. She had a "braiding" room set up just off the front entryway. I made myself comfortable, looking at her photo albums of styles. It was obvious to me that she could do all sorts of styles and all sorts of braids. There were individuals, cornrows, coils, Nubian knots, Cassimas, thick, small and everything in between. I was excited!!!.

I settled on my usual style - single medium sized braids and promised myself that the next time I need a special occasion **"Do"** I would come to her.

We watched TV, chatted and snacked as she braided. During our noon break I excused myself to the restroom. I was sure she must be at least half way through. She wasn't!!! I took a look at my head in the bathroom mirror and realized she wasn't even a third complete!! Oh My GOD!!! How long was this going to take??? I wasn't sure what to say or do. Actually I realized there wasn't much I could do but to let her finish.

Well, as you can guess, finishing took a while. **TEN HOURS** to be exact!!!! My butt was numb. I was tired and hungry. I paid her $100 fee. Thinking to my self was the reduction in what I had paid Maxine worth the four plus hours additional in time?? NOT!!!!

I said thank-you and good-bye, got in the car and called Kathy from my cell phone. Kathy could not believe I was just getting done.... "There is no way I am going to this women," she said. Well,she did. We were still having difficulty finding someone so she did not have a choice.

Finally…while at lunch one day I noticed a sister with a very nice braid job. YES!! I thought…. a possibility. One would think it would be difficult to approach a total stranger and ask about her hair. In general, this is not the case for sisters needing a new "Do". Our appearance is paramount …our hair even more so. Therefore, saying to a sister **"You are looking Good Girl, who did your hair!"**, is considered a compliment and something you would want to answer and probably discuss in detail.

This was the case that afternoon. I introduced myself explaining that I was on the hunt for a braider. Turned out that her braider was her daughter! GREAT!!! I had hit the jackpot. We exchanged the pertinent information and goodbyes. With a lilt in my step I made a beeline to the telephone to call Kathy.

Niki was a great find. She was a young single mom who was supplementing her income as an insurance representative by braiding. Kathy was the first to have her hair braided by Niki. I went along for moral support.

Niki was sharing a three-bedroom first floor apartment with her mother, brother and 8-month-old son. He was a great baby but turned out to be a handful while she tried to braid. We chatted, had lunch, watched **B.E.T** and generally had a great time, while Niki braided Kathy's hair. It took her 5 hours to complete. Not bad and the end result was wonderful!!

Niki became **"our"** braider from that point on. So, for about six months I would go to Niki to have my hair braided. Soon my hair got long enough for me to do on my own. I saved a lot of money and had the added satisfaction of saying I had braided my hair on my own.

During this period I started noticing something. **LOCKS**...lots and lots of LOCKS!! I would have thoughts like...**"I wonder what I would look like with Dread-Locks?**

I found myself devouring Braid Magazines; with the specific focus on locating any and all information about locking. I was nervous about the prospect but very intrigue by the "Look". There was something about people that had their hair locked that I wouldn't quite put my finger on. Something Spiritual. Who ever I saw with locks seemed peaceful, serene, focused and strong. I looked at Toni Morrison, Lauren Hill, Alice Walker, Cassandra Wilson and Lenny Kravits, they all had that **"Something"**.

I started cutting out pictures and articles from the braid magazines. Occasionally there was a great article about natural hair/locking. I bought books; <u>Good Hair</u> & <u>Platied Glory</u> by Lonnice Brittenum Bonner; <u>No Lye! The African-American Woman's Guide to Natural Hair Care by,</u> Tulani Knard; and finally, <u>Everything You Need to Know About Hairlocking</u> by Nekhena Evans. I would read each book in one sitting and often re-read them to gain deeper and continued understanding.

I was fascinated by the idea of allowing my hair to be what it was naturally was meant to be. No additives ...chemicals or hair!! **Nothing!! Just my own crown and glory! Nappy as I want to be!**

I considered just doing the natural twist. I considered doing the **"twist and finger it out"** look. I considered going back to an Afro. But none of these is what I really wanted. I really wanted to lock. But I didn't have the **guts.**

In the summer of 1998 we took our usual family vacation to Martha's Vineyard. Yep! The Vineyard. For those of you who don't know there is a large African-American community on the Island. There has been this presence on the Vineyard for Centuries, but many "folk" don't know about it. We love going for the sense of community and ethnic connectedness one feels while on the beach or walking the streets of Oak Bluffs. Our kids have made friends that they see year after year. Friends we know they will maintain as they grow-up when they bring their on kids to the island.

Kathy's family vacations there as well. We usually see one another several times during the day while on the island. One afternoon we were leaving one of the stores on Circuit Avenue, when we saw this sister with locks down her back. She was dressed in Afro- centric clothing and looking every bit the African Queen. There was a regal quality about her. We followed her back in the store. She was with some girlfriends. I approached her. **"Sister, your locks are beautiful…how long have you been growing them?"** Her friend quickly interjected**" they are beautiful, but I am not ready"** I thought to myself…I wasn't talking to you!!! The sister with the locks turned towards me and with not a smile or a sense of warmth (guess I was wrong about the warmth thing!!) she said five years and turned back towards the jewelry she was examining. I felt dismissed!!! I thought " did I do something wrong?" I am sure it was at that pointed that I decided that when I have my locks…for I knew it was just a matter of time…I would be open and supportive to those who inquired. I also knew **I was not ready yet.**

I continued my quest for information about locking, as I continued to braid my hair. My braiding got better and better and I knew my head was looking good…but I still was into the, **I want to lock but not ready thing!!**

I decided to do a little searching on the Web. I located a site from a gentleman in Sweden!! **Sweden!!** I know what you are thinking…yep!! He was a Swede and his site was extremely informative. I learned much about the spiritual connection and the many tribes of people all over the world that locked their hair. The one thing that stuck with me was that those of European descent who wanted to lock had to **"destroy their hair".**

On the site there were instructions to use laundry detergent and other solutions to strip the hair of its natural resources. Amazing!!! The site went on to explain that those of African descent just had to allow their hair to **"be"** and the locks would come.!!

In the spring of 1999 I had the opportunity to do some work on the island of St. Croix. I was excited…not only was I going to get paid for working in an American paradise but I had the opportunity to see a friend.

Aminah is from St Croix, but grew up in NYC most of her life. She returned to St Croix with her family some years ago. When I telephoned her with my plans she immediately said that I had to spend some time with her.

I arrived two days before my scheduled work was to begin. Aminah met me at the airport. My plane landed, I went through customs, exited the restricted area and saw her walking towards me. There she was!! And she had **LOCKS!!!!** We screamed, hugged and laughed…it was great to see one another. The next thing out of my mouth was, "You locked your hair…**it's beautiful"…"I've been thinking about locking!"**

As we walked toward the parked car she told me how she had been thinking about locking for sometime herself. Then one night after shampooing, she just started twisting her hair and that was it. She explained how easy it was and how she **"now had a relationship with her hair that she never had before".** It was of positive relationship **"Sharon, I love my hair!!"**. Wow what a statement.. I love my hair". I thought about that for sometime as we rode to her home. The sun was beautiful, the palm trees were swaying we played catch up on our lives. All the while I was thinking, "I don't think I have ever truly <u>loved</u> my hair. I loved some of the styles I've had….love it??…not really!!. Is this what locking does to you????

During my stay with Aminah I met a few of her sister-friends all of whom had their hair locked. Of course each head was beautiful and full of life. That's it!! There was life in those heads!!! I could see it in every single individual lock. Some stood tall, some curled and some had these amazing angles. It didn't matter, they all had <u>life</u>. Aminah's, Barbara's' and Yamaya's, all of them beautiful!!

I continued contemplating, but not for long. As I asked these women questions and absorbed their answers and wisdom I was clear. My decision was made! I was ready; I was going to lock my hair!! I decided that when it was time to take out my newly braided hair I would double twist and begin the journey!!!

So, on August 25, 1999 while on vacation on Martha's Vineyard, I twisted my hair!! I was a nervous wreck! It looked strange, felt strange and I was sure people were staring at me!

But you know what?? It felt great!! Liberating. I remembered something an acquaintance said…. you just have to work with it girl!! So I worked with it! I used scarves and headbands. I bought great earrings. In other words "I tried to love my hair". But it wasn't working.

I found myself questioning what was I doing. I was nervous about going out in public. So, after my two weeks at the Vineyard I decided to take out the twist. I was going to do my locks in a less obvious way. I was going to lock while I had extensions in! I think I remember someone saying this was a possibility. I figured no problem. I decided it wasn't necessary to remove the twist I had. During the twisting process I had decided it made sense not to comb out the hair that had been braided with extensions. I figured this would give my hair a great start in the locking process. Particularly since locking was about allowing your hair to be nappy. And believe me after having your hair braid for 2 to 3 months it was NAPPY!!

So, if I just used the now twisted hair as the third piece of hair to be braided into an extension, I was sure

I could have my cake and eat it to. ...NAPPIN UP LOCKS WITH Long FLOWING BRAIDS!!

Deep down inside I felt like there was something wrong with my inability to just let my hair <u>be</u>. Maybe I wasn't ready after all!! Oh well !! I decided so what…you do what you have to do!!

I purchased some #2 human braiding hair and began the process of braiding. It was going pretty well and didn't take as long as I thought it would. When complete, I looked in the mirror and admired my handy work. Huh!! It looked fine…. So why wasn't I ecstatic?? Didn't I now have my cake?? But eating it wasn't as appealing!! <u>I WAS A SELL OUT</u>!!!! Having locks was about something else. I wasn't sure what it was, but it wasn't this.

The next day I took the braids out. I can handle this? I know I can ! *I said as I tried to convince myself!* For the next couple of weeks I managed to deal with it. I was still self-conscious when in pubic. At home was a different story.

My husband was quasi-supportive. "It looks ok" he'd say and then in the next breath "now when is it going to lock". My youngest just said, "I hope you are not going on the cruise next year looking like that!" I continued to worry with my vanity getting the best of me.

In October while shopping for some hair products, I spotted a wig. It was a dreadlock Fall! It had a headband that when pushed back just enough the locks looked as if they were coming from your own head. Now I could work with this!!! This was the best of both worlds.

I purchased the fall and started to wear it immediately! Everyone thought it was my hair!! I was still feeling a little guilty but not enough to give it up!

I decided I would wear it the following weekend to a Sinbad concert at the local university. As we took our seats several people commented on how beautiful my locks were. I graciously said thank-you as my husband looked at me with this knowing grin. I was beginning to feel uncomfortable. Actually, I felt like a fraud! At the intermission I caught a glimpse of myself in the window. My reflection appeared to say back to me..."Lookin good Girl......even if it isn't your own hair" Once again I realized, I must not be truly ready!!

That following week I had a lunch date planned with a good friend, - some one I had not seen a months. We decided to meet at a local Caribbean restaurant. We both loved the food there! I arrived about ten minutes early. The waitress showed me to my table. As she handed me the menu she said "Oh your locks are beautiful" and before I could respond she went on to say how she wanted to lock but had not gotten the nerve. I shared with her that locking is indeed a process. Not only the actually cultivation of the locks but the emotional process was a difficult one. And before I realized it, I said, "This is a wig, I am locking underneath it". I had no idea I would share that detail with anyone. Was this a sign that I was inching along to acceptance?

I spotted Gloria as she placed coins in the meter across the street. Were those locks?? !!! As she walked closer, it was confirmed she was locking! How long had it been since I had seen her. Six, eight months I thought to myself. Gloria walked in to the restaurant and we greeted one another with a big hug, simultaneously marveling at the fact that we were both locking.

"Oh my GOD Sharon, look at your hair" she said. I immediately told her it was a wig and that I was indeed in the process of locking! We had a wonderful time. In confessing my struggle with accepting my hair she validated all my feelings of fear, shame and pride. I left that lunch knowing that I needed to remove the wig…but how was I going to get the courage and isn't there something wrong with a need to have courage to show your hair for what it is??? I was confused but less so than prior to walking in that restaurant. Some how the waitress and Gloria had made an impact on me. A nudge that was moving me in a direction I know I <u>wanted</u> and <u>needed</u> to go. Once again I asked myself "Are you ready"!

But of course I was ready!!! I just had to really take a look at my reasons for wanting to lock my hair. What were they??? There was of course the sense of pride, a connection to my roots. There was the ease of locks (or so I thought…. no fuss no muss…get up and go hair!! That was extremely enticing.

But there was something else I needed to confront. It was the European esthetic of beauty. The idea that "behaving hair" was hair that laid-down, and did what you wanted; Was that what locks did! But locks did <u>not</u> lie down…especially in their infancy. They stood up and seemed to say "Hey take notice!!!"

I remembered something I learned in a self-improvement seminar. It had to do with dealing with relationships. It went something like this...

"Love them for who they are and who they aren't"

That was it!! I had to let go of my idea of a behaving, <u>idealistic</u> relationship with my hair and move to an alive, vibrant and <u>loving</u> relationship with my hair.

I had to change my relationship with my hair. I had to cleanse myself of the negative messages about African Hair!! Funny thing is, I thought I had done that when I started wearing a Fro and extensions. I guess I was now faced with a new level of understanding, a new level of honesty and true love of my GOD given strength!! MY HAIR as it was meant to be! My Antennae to GOD! I realized there is power in this head. There is an aliveness that is difficult to explain. At that moment of true acceptance I crossed over. I Crossed over into a "KNOWING" and a "LOVING " of my hair.

No more wigs, no nothing. I truly felt
liberated this time. It was for real.

So began my true odyssey with the process of locking my hair. I had read all there was to read…now it was time to "<u>Do</u>" the relationship.

Finding the right products to use was a process. I had read some conflicting information. One that said it didn't matter another that said no products with alcohol in them and of course no cream based products. Still others said stay away from beeswax. And yet another said stick with natural products. I read that locks love hot oil treatments and another that said stay away from oiling your hair period…. only place oil on the scalp!!!

Then there was the issue of washing. There was everything from don't wash after you first prepare the "buds" for an entire month; to wash every couple of weeks. What was a sistah to do!!! I thought this was supposed to be easy!!!!

I decided I knew my hair best. I had spent a lifetime with it, even if the relationship had been one of struggle! My soft, fine hair absorbed moisture. Therefore, I figured I should wash it as often as I normally did...every two weeks. I was sure this would help with the locking processes. After each washing I did a hot oil treatment of a mixture of essential oils and olive oil.

I reviewed the books I had purchased and decided I would go the "as natural as possible" route with products. I had read in a past Essences magazine that Carol's Daughter products were the best. Noted stars like Eryca Badu, Lauryen Hill and Eric Benet' used her products. If they were good enough for them they certainly were good enough for me.

My first order included "Loc Butter", Ocean Shampoo and Herbal Rinse , Hair Balm and Khoret Amen Oil. They all smelled wonderful!! Good enough to eat actually!

Every evening I oiled my scalp with the Khoret Amen oil and alternated between the Hair Balm and Loc Butter on the locks themselves. And of course before going to bed I put my "Do Rag" on!

Occasionally I would substitute Dr. Bonners Peppermint Castile Soap and St Ives Moisturizing Shampoo for the Carol's Daughter products. They were both filled with all natural ingredients and no alcohol. I continue this routine almost three years later!

I figure this might be a good place to share with you my stages of Locking. In the book "Everything You Need to Know About Hairlocking" by Nekhena Evans there is a wonderful definition of hairlocking. "Hairlocking is a biological process which occurs when naturally coiled or spiraled hair (black people's hair type) is allowed to develop in its natural state, without combing or the use of chemicals. The hair will go through progressive stages of interlocking and coiling similar to DNA replication, until it finally becomes a dense tight Lock i.e. tress. The hairlocking process usually takes an average of six months to a year to complete. Once this process is complete the hair is locked and cannot be combed or loosened without being severed."[2]

Wow, six months to a year!! As I read that I thought 'No Way", my hair when left to its own devises would surely lock over night!! Well...ok...if not overnight surely it would lock in a few months!! I was totally disbelieving that there were stages to locking. These stages I would later learn, not only represented the stages of hair growth but my spiritual growth and connection to my hair as well.

Nekhena describes four stages of the locking process. They are:

Pre-Lock Phase- the hair is in thin tightly coiled spirals. Its appearance is along the lined of either ringlets or Shirley Temple curls. This is the infancy stage (baby locks).

---

[2] Evans, Nekhena. Everything You Need To Know About Hairlocking, Brooklyn, New York A &B Publishers Group 1996 pg. XIII

Budding Phase- during this phase a small bud (like a pea in a pod) begins to emerge about three quarters down the lock. The matted interlocking imprint begins at the bud and then expands like a bubble because it is beginning to loosely mat. It is an enlarged microcosm of a lock. At this stage the lock is no longer tight and thin. It is rebellious, has a mind of its own and is discovering its own way (teen lock), It acts like a teenager in a sense.

Shooting Phase- After the budding, the entire lock begins a process of interlocking and matting. The direction is downward from the bud to the end of the hair and back upwards toward the scalp (similar to how plants develop). The hair closest to the scalp is not locked; this is where you have new growth. During this phase, the hair increases in density because it begins to replicate itself like DNA. Your hair remains in this phase for the longest period of time (adult locks)

Contracting Phase- This is the final stage in which the hair becomes mature adult locks; airtight interlocked, spiraling, network system. The locks become consistent, tight and fairly solid at this point, as the hair will grow extraordinarily once the spiral form has been established (elder locks)[3]

It only makes sense to lead you through my journey of these particular stages.... My pre-lock stage was, how should I say, ...interesting. Yep, interesting.

I couldn't decide if I love it or hated it. It looked disorganized, unkempt with very little body to it. But

---

[3] Evans, Nekhena,. Everything You Need to Know About Hairlocking, Brooklyn, New York A&B Publishers Group 1996, pg 18

there was something about them that I thought was cute.

My new two strand twists were thin, kind of curly mini little…"things". I was sure it would not take long for them to lock. To my surprise it took at least a couple of months before I saw the "bud" or pea form in my locks. And actually it did not form in all of them at the same time. Somehow I thought there would be some uniformity to this locking thing!

The Budding stage finally began to occur. I am sure that it was during this stage I began to "know" each one of my locks. I found my self fingering, smoothing, and caressing each one as I attempted to get to know its character and personality. It was at this point that I also understood two things. One…. my hair was not the same all over my head. As the old folks would say I had a "different grade of hair" on the top that was different from the sides that was different from the back! Although softer and a bit curlier than the top and sides…the back of my hair locked and grew faster.

Second, this was indeed the rebellious Teen stage that Nekhena mentioned! There were many days that no matter what I did, a lock or two would misbehave! I mean…just do whatever it wanted. Stand straight at attention; appear curly at a rather interesting angle, flop in my face. I could talk to them, attempt to reason with them, punish them!! It didn't matter that just did what they wanted to. Finally I realized that if I let them be with some occasional guidance they would settle down and mature.

It did not take long for my rebellious teen locks to get a grip!! My shooting stage began about six to eight months into the process. This is the stage that I remained in for the longest. My hair started to look less curly, less ringlets… and more like locks. They started to get thicker, fatter, and denser. They obeyed now, having settled down. I felt a sort of regal quality I hadn't felt until this stage. There was a connection that I was feeling that emanated throughout my body. I loved to touch, watch it, experience it and yes even explain it to others. I started noticing others noticing them. I felt a specialness about my hair I had never felt before.

It is difficult to pinpoint when my locks matured. When I was locking I was spending so much time in the initial stages comparing mine to someone else's. Mine were not long enough, thick enough, or pretty enough. As I looked to my first "**Lock-Anniversary,**" I realized something. At some point my spiritual connection to them matured and I was no longer after someone else's "spirit" but loving and accepting my own. As I reflect, I think that was the point my locks started to mature. They began to flourish. All of a sudden I realized I could pull them back in a small ponytail.

My locks are mature now. Or should I say maturing. For I feel as they grow so do I. It has been 2 plus years now. I am at the Contracting stage. They are solid and beautiful. I even started getting new ones!! I was shocked that I could develop new locks. Somehow, I thought the locks you started with were all you get. But as all things grow, new things develop and so…in the midst of maturing locks I have <u>new budding locks, wild and rebellious teen locks.</u>

<u>I THINK I'm STARTING A FAMILY!!</u>

Kathy's Journey

"At Least now I can exhale!"

Kathy is more to me than a friend. There really aren't words that adequately describe our connection. We often joke about "how it (our relationship) was meant to be". Kathy IS MY SISTER!! Bloodlines could not have provided me with someone more sister-like than she. There is indeed something extraordinarily special about a relative of choice!!!

We are so connected that I am sure you noticed that it was impossible for me to write my own story without including her! Therefore I won't rehash what you already know; but I will share with you some things you don't.

Kathy has had her hair "natural" for 5 years. She has been locking since June 2001.

Her Journey to the locking process has often paralleled my own. Or should I say my journey has paralleled hers.... that is until I made the leap first to lock my hair!

One thing about Kathy and her hair that stood out for me early in our relationship is how good her haircuts looked on her.

And the color!!! I always wished I could add blond highlights to my hair! Not withstanding that it would have looked like crap!! Nonetheless, I envied those highlights!

I remember one time when Kathy had a hair coloring, highlighting fiasco. It required hours to do and double the hours and process to correct before the brassy orange color was relegated to something more natural! Oh the pain of it all. "Oh my GOD, Sharon I look like Bozo the clown!" We both wondered if the corrective process would result in baldness! It didn't!

Kathy's head has seen it all. It's been permed, wigged, cut, twisted, afro-ed, braided, extended, curled, pressed, straightened…and anything else you can think of.

Five years ago she decided to let her perm grow out so she could once again have it braided with extensions. Mind you, she did not let me know of this decision until AFTER I had my hair trimmed so close you couldn't even grab it between two fingers and re-permed at a local Beauty School!! Oh well!

Looking back she never had an inkling that this decision would lead to locks five years later. Braids would allow for a rest, and increase her style options.

A few years of braided hair that required numerous hunts for braiders and hair for that matter became a catalyst for the "True Naps discussion" between us. The thinking about locks and the honest talk began. But before moving on let me share the "human hair for braiding hunt".

Finding quality human hair requires energy that is difficult to explain. There is a diligence and education that is needed to find the right shade, brand, weight and texture. You will travel, by foot, car, train and even utilize the Internet to get the best deal.

Kathy and I always shared any new deals. We went from Blue Hills Ave, to Main Street Hartford, to "Beauty Enterprise" and "Sally's Beauty Products". We drove to New Haven and hit all the shops on the upper end of Chapel Street to the "hood" shops (some owned by Asians) on Dixwell Avenue. Our hunt even took us to New York City the "Big Apple" had lots "Big-Hair" resources. From 125th street in Harlem to Nina's in Midtown Manhattan to an occasional trip to Fulton Street in Brooklyn. We were bound by our desire to have the best deal. It became apparent that the best deal was a little shop off 28th street between 6th and 7th Aves in Manhattan. So good was the deal that we bought hair wholesale and sold to friends and acquaintances. That didn't last too long…too much work!! So we would plan our purchases around our needs and buy in bulk on an as needed basis.

Ok…now back to the "Naps Discussion".

As I said, a few years of braided extensions gets you to thinking. We were noticing more and more truly nappy heads. Yes, we saw twist and Afros but we also saw "lots of locks". Our on and off discussion about locks began. The most difficult thing was about the <u>commitment</u>. A decision to lock was more than a style it was a way of Being. Kathy wasn't ready.

"Since I had braids, I guess my hair was considered in its natural state.

NOT!!!

My hair was not in the true sense of the word natural. I had someone else's hair intertwined with my own hair. I guess that could be considered as rather unnatural."

" Before beginning my journey my relationship with my hair was not a loving one. It did not allow freedom. It was truly a love/hate relationship. When I thought it was working for me I loved it. And when it didn't I wanted it to change, be like something else. Not ever allowing it to be itself. As if it couldn't be beautiful unto itself."

Thinking back to the pain of "unnatural" hair. Kathy shared the following. "Pain!!...I'll share my pain! Burning my forehead, ears, fingers and back of the neck. Trying to look like my friends in the 60's during the British invasion by wearing a rather stupid looking Beatle wig. (You had to grow up in my neighborhood to understand!) That pain resulted in my wanting to be me! To have ownership...for me to have control of me"

"My husband has responded to my new natural hair with the support of ...*you look good in anything you wear honey.*

My mother-in-law stated oh, you changed your hair again. Well if you don't like it, your hair grows fast anyway when you cut it."

"My co-workers...oh, that looks cute (that response is expected since I still have the curly/twisty end thing going on)...it looks like Shirley Temple curls. Do you think I can do that to my hair? Is it going to stay like that??"

"People of color have been mostly positive. Often stating they would like to be natural but need courage. They would like to but can't."

"Having a best friend to share my hair raising experiences has been exhilarating and uplifting. The two of us taking turns being the guinea pig trying to find the right "Do"...at least for the moment any way. Having her lead the way to my freedom...at last!

"At least now I can exhale!!"

Sesheta-Nai's Story

"Mommy you hurt my mind when you comb my hair"

I met *Nai* (as her family calls her) at our first "Nappy & Happy" conference in the spring of 2000. She was six years old.

At first sight, one is drawn to the <u>spirit</u> of this little girl. There is indeed an aura about Nai. Strength of purpose, a clearness of who she is and what she is, emanates from her. This is strange to see projected in such a young child.

Her mother, Jennifer tells me Nai was almost five when she uttered those profound words, ("Mommy you hurt my mind when you comb my hair!". Nai and her mother share her story with me.

Jennifer and her husband were clear about one thing as it related to their daughter. She would not have her hair straightened! When she was old enough they would allow her to decide how she wanted to wear her hair. …. Straightening it was not an option.

One day as Jennifer was combing her daughter's thick beautifully kinky hair, Nai said…."Mommy you hurt my mind when you comb my hair". It was clear the day had come for Nai to decide how she wanted to wear her hair. Jennifer gave Nai a choice "you could have it cut to a very close Natural like mine or you can grow locks. Nai choose locks!! So locks it would be!!

During the interview I asked Nai why she wanted to lock her hair? She responded in a typical childlike way "I don't know?" her mom then asked, "Do you remember what it was like when I use to comb your hair?" Nai did not verbally respond but her face told the story. There was a "scared" look …one that spoke volumes. "

When Jennifer told me this all I could say was "Wow!!! How deep a statement that was. It resonated with me!. How much had my mind been hurt as a result of the combing, abuse and self-abuse that had been inflicted upon my hair? I wondered aloud "How different my sense of self-worth, identity and beauty might have been if I had a mother who thought and responded like Jennifer had?" The sense of empowerment was overwhelming. I was jealous! It had taken me almost 50 years to get where this little girl was!

Nai attracts attention in ways her parents never thought would occur due to her locks. There are several male neighbors who have locked hair that Nai makes a point of saying hello to everyday. They respond to her in an affirming manner. "My teacher Miss Johnson has locks" another affirming, positive role model.

Of course there are times Nai's parents are questioned about why they locked their daughter's hair "Why would you do that to her", as if there was something being done to her that was negative and potentially harmful. Nai's parents are quick to respond by letting them know that this was her decision not theirs.

Nai now seven is as strong as ever. Recently her mother related this story. "Nai is the only child in her school who is locked. And has been for the last 3 years. On picture day a little Chinese girl said to Nai "didn't you know it is picture day?...you didn't do your hair!' Nai responded. "My hair is done" and kept on walking! She has gotten to the point where she doesn't want me to groom them. I'll ask her do you want me to pull them back. Her response to me is no, leave them alone they are done.

Nai is currently contemplating cutting her locks so that she can join her mother in the locking process. Jennifer says Nai continues to encourage and support her. "There are times I just want to go wash it out...and Nai will say no mommy don't do that"

Jennifer's Journey
"I am looking to Grow with my locks"

Jennifer, Nai's mother has had her hair natural for about 5 years. She is about 8 weeks into the process of locking. When I first interviewed Jennifer she wore her hair in a very close cropped natural.

"I could not bear to sit in the beauty salon for 3-4 hours when I could be spending that time with my children, or sleeping or anything. I hated listening to the gossip. I did not want my ears burnt to a crisp under the dryers anymore. I did not want to deal with hairdressers that never even smiled even though they were getting my money. I decided that I could use the $65(plus tip) for a full perm and $35(plus tip) for a touch up, for more meaningful things. I knew that after all that the hairdo would look like crap the very next day. I also knew that rain had become my worse enemy."

Her natural close-cropped style required little work. " I hardly had to think about my hair. I sat in the barber's chair for 30 minutes with his undivided attention. When done I received daily compliments on my hair. Before I decided to go natural I hated my hair. I had no clue as to how to style it. I hated the fact that I had to deal with it at all. I used to wear it in a ponytail or with a single cornrow down the back with bangs in the front. I despised "new growth"(which would require a touch up)"

"When I decide to go the natural route my mother thought I'd go back to permming after a few months. When she found out I was not she told me I should get it permed at the length I wear it. I asked her what was the point? She had no answer.

"My friends encouraged me once I" threatened" to do it. They were very supportive. I had not warned my husband that I was going to cut my hair off. So when he got home he looked puzzled and said 'that's nice". I knew he didn't mean it."

Her cropped style got the following responses from others.

"Men with locks seem to be very attracted to me. I once asked one man who felt this attraction, why? He said because women that wear their hair like this have a greater confidence level than women who use chemicals.

European descent women seemed to love it and the freedom they perceived it provided. European descent men usually didn't comment. It appeared as if they were thinking nice thoughts but dare not say anything."

"Other women of color usually complimented me on the shape of my head and the shortness of my hair. They say they would love to be able to get up the nerve to cut their hair but for many reasons they held back. Here are some of the reasons I've heard:

- My man loves my hair long (and straight)!
- My employer wouldn't approve!
- My kids would be upset!
- My family would disown me!
- My face is too big!
- My hair is too nappy under the perm!
- My head is funny shaped!
- I am scared I wont like it.!

Jennifer could identify with some of these reasons. She went on to share. "When I worked in corporate America I used to try to make sure my hair was perfect so I could fit in with the people who had naturally straight hair. I felt they would not accept me if my hair was a 'mess" or if it was not perfectly done everyday

Jennifer has now entered new stage of growth as it relates to her hair. She has decided to Lock. She attributes this decision to two things...her daughter, and her attendance at the Nappy & Happy Conference.

"I look at my daughter and I want to be like her.... have that confidence." When I first started to lock I didn't want anyone to see me like this. Nai and my husband have encouraged me. He told me, Jennifer, you have to take this step.

Jennifer has been stepping ever since. There are times she is frustrated with what to do with it. Concerned about how often she should wash it. Looking for a remedy for the itching and flaking but she is not giving in. "I realize that this is a process. I want to grow with my locks."

Kelly V's Journey
"The Re-Birth of Nap"

"Until last Christmas, my 85 year-old grandmother and I feuded for five years over whether black is beautiful. She is a short, dark woman, with kinky, gray hair who has been trying for seven decades to lighten her skin. When I wanted to hit below the belt, I would remind her that Michael Jackson had unlocked the secrets of skin whitening and suggest that she contact him for advice."

'For four years, the gist of Grandma's argument was that I should straighten the nappy Afro I was growing. I had stopped straightening my hair when I went away to college because I was tired of trying to conform to white standards for female beauty."

Grandma's arguments were so patently racist she sounded like the deceased founder of the Klu Klux Klan, Nathan Bedford Forrest, had possessed her. Her mouth didn't froth or anything, but often she'd narrow her beady eyes and upchuck a "loogie" on my black pride and me. "Black people look like monkeys", she would say. "Everybody knows white women are the most beautiful women on the face of this planet."

My nappy Afro had dashed my hopes of ever watching TV in peace at her house. Then at Christmas 1999, I inadvertently cast a spell over her that forced Nathan Bedford Forest to retreat. I got dreadlocks."

I had started locking my Afro a few weeks after visiting her the previous Christmas. I could tell she loved my new look. "What's that called?' She asked, frowning. "Locks," I said. "You like it?"…"looks all right," she mumbled and we watched the rest of the "Family Feud" in silence.

While the views my Grandmother expressed dismayed me, they were reasonable for someone whose black features have been subjected to 85 years of white ridicule. Tell a person she's a monkey long enough and threaten to lynch her if she doesn't believe you. It's strange how she will start to agree.

To mitigate white reproach and the reproach of brainwashed fellow blacks, African Americans have been covering their kinky hair, gelling it straight with animal fat, or frying it straight with hot combs and chemical relaxers since the inception of slavery.

"Black women straightened their hair to survive" said stylist Michelle Robinson of Oakland California, who now has locked hair. "we had to work in white folks' houses. Who was going to let us do that with a nappy head of hair?"

Then, during the Black Power Movement of the 1960s, the unprocessed Afro became a common black style. When the movement dissipated, many black women returned to straightening their hair.

But in the past five years, particularly in urban areas, large numbers of black women and men have begun to embrace natural hair again. Chemical relaxer sales have been in a slump since 1997, according to market analyst Packaged Facts, who attribute the product's sluggish sales to "the popularity of low maintenance natural (unprocessed) looks", as it was during the Black Power Movement, it's now hip to be nappy. And dreadlocks. Or more precisely—their manicured cousins, twisted locks—seem to be at the forefront of this development.

In Black Neighborhoods across America, salons and stylists specializing in hair locking are cropping up everywhere. Go into a beauty supply store serving black communities and vying for shelf space with the hair straighteners, you will find any of five new pomades released within the past five years for locking black hair.

"Four years ago, there were two salons in Baltimore that locked hair", said Tyra Jackson, the maker of the pomade Princess Kayla's Natty Dreadlock. "Now there are over 20, all of which sell Princess Kayla. "Jackson retails her product through 80 vendors, including the California-based, upscale health food chain store, Whole foods.

In addition, to Baltimore the upsurge in hair locking is apparent in the San Francisco Bay Area, Los Angeles, New York, Washington D.C. and Atlanta, where salons and stylists who pioneered twisted locks originated the style. When I asked the founding mothers (most of the stylist are women) to disclose their business' sales, they all demurred. But they eagerly assured me business was booming. "We work hard every single day!" said Rasario Schuler-Ukpabi, the proprietor of the Oakland based, Oh! My Nappy Hair.

No doubt about it, twisted locks have arrived. But why and where are they going? The question gnawing at the souls of lock-wearers, the wallets of "locticians", and the minds of observers of popular culture is whether locks have staying power. Are locks just another fad, the Afro-centric equivalent of the now "uber-passe", Regan-era Jheri Curl? Or do locks reflect a permanent, metaphysical shift in Black consciousness?

Three Buppies and a Mercedes:

Every "loctician" that I talked to said they were creating a permanent shift in black consciousness by locking people's hair. But when I asked Stanford historian Kennell Jackson whether the recent upsurge in hair locking reflected a permanent shift in Black consciousness, he mocked my question by asking me to clarify the definition of "locks".

"What are you talking about?" said Professor Jackson, a bald, distinguished black man who chronicles black popular culture. "You talking about buppy dreads? Because that's what I call them. It came to me when I was vacationing in Sea Ranch, California and saw a black family with manicured dreadlocks getting into their Mercedes. "Twisted locks are an adaptation of the cultivated dreadlock to the black urban professional's (buppy) predominantly corporate work environment, Professor Jackson said.

Indeed, the adaptation seems necessary for the buppy's survival. When a 1981 New York court upheld American Airlines' dismissal of a black flight attendant who styled her hair in cornrows, it gave employers the green light to fire employees based on hairstyle.

"As long as a company's policy is evenhanded: Berkeley law professor Angela Harris explained" i.e. apples to all races and genders, that company can ban cornrows or dreadlocks." (Before you say "but people of all races don't wear cornrows," think: Bo Derrick. According to the New York court, the flight attendant's cornrows were little more than a Bo Derrick-inspired fad)

Twisted locks are cultivated by parting an Afro into squares whose sides are roughly the length of a nickel. Pomade is applied to one square at a time to condition the hair and help it stick together. Then each square is combed into a Shirley Temple curl, or twist.

One month later the hair is washed, it reverts to an Afro, and the process must be repeated. Except this time, when a section of hair is twisted into the Shirley temple Curl, the tips of the curl will have become matted. These matted tips will not be disturbed and any loose hairs adjacent to a tip will be gelled to the tip with pomade. Whenever the hair is washed, it will be re-twisted in this fashion. Overtime these tips bud and become mature locks.

Under the guidance of a stylist, developing nature twisted locks takes 6-12 months and $45-$75 dollars per wash and re-twist. Contrast this elaborate, potentially costly process with the method for growing uncultivated dreadlocks and you'll understand why professor Jackson calls twisted locks buppy dreadlocks. Uncultivated dreadlocks are a wash and go style whose development some wearers accelerate with beeswax. But curly hair dreads are naturally - no maintenance is required. Bob Marley's prescription for growing Dreadlocks. "Trust the universe enough to respect your hair."

"I can't say that this is a shift in consciousness, " Professor Jackson said about twisted locks. There's no real uproar over it. You see people with locks on commercials of mainstream products," he noted referring to ads for brands such as Gap, Kodak, and Lysol. "Keep in mind: advertising is risk averse"

"There are no new premises behind locking," Professor Jackson added. The Afro, on the one hand, was a backlash against whitewashed images of black beauty projected by the media, he said." Locking is at most a continuation of the legacy of the Black Power Movement."

Blacker Than Thou

Quantitatively, it is difficult to gauge the Black Power Movement's imprint on black's aesthetic sensibilities. After the Movement dissipated, black women were running after the relaxer kits like Marion Jones to the 400-meters finish line. During the 80's, sales of relaxers grew at a rate of 10 percent per year…far out pacing the concomitant growth in black population…according to marketing analyst - Packaged Facts.

Although the Afro's popularity faded, its influence on the politics of black identity did not, said Harold Thomas of New York's Locks and Chops, the shop that pioneered the twisted lock. "Generations of black people have become conscious of their identities, of the falseness that has been perpetrated on them. Those beauty myths have been demystified,' Mr. Thomas said.

Loctician Michelle Robinson, who has about 100 regular clients, agrees. "The Afro was important," she said of the vaunted symbol of Black Power. But Ms. Robinson insists that twisted locks are not a simple extension of the Afro's legacy. "The Afro didn't stick because it wasn't personal. This time, locking hair, just going natural period, is not political…it's purely spiritual. Its about self-esteem, self awareness, and self-respect," she said,

One of Michelle's clients, a male, described the psychological benefits of locking his hair in the testimonial he offered on her website; "I've gotten to grow inside out. The growing process has given me the true vision of myself. I wear my locks with the strength and the power that comes along with true knowledge of self."

Either way, I know one old lady who, because of locks, is a little prouder to be black today than she was five years ago. Last Christmas when I visited her, my grandmother slightly upgraded her approval of my locks. She thumbed through my hair with upturned mouth and nose, inspecting my now shoulder length locks. "Look pretty good," she said. "Look pretty good".

Michelle's Journey
"I Like your Hair"

There is a strong countenance about Michelle. A spiritual quiet that seems ever present. That was my first impression of her. And it remains today!! Michelle is a Professor at small New England well known college. So one can imagine the beauty and strength of this women as she walks the hallowed halls with her beautiful head of sun kissed locks. Now that's POWER!!!

I had not seen Michelle in at least four years. For awhile I maintained contact through BIRG(Black Issues Research Group) a list serve that Michelle started that is dedicated to the intellectual discussion about current events , personal issues, support and validation to those of us in academia and those of us that like to contribute to the discussion. At some point…probably during the many quests my husband and I have had to find a server that doesn't constantly drop your connection…I got disconnected from the group.

In June 2001 we reconnected. I was attending the Middletown High School graduation of the class of 2001. My husband as chairman of the board was to address the class and hand out the diplomas (He always jokes about how when the family members look at the photos of the graduate receiving the diploma, they would ask who is that Black man!!) I was attending to bear witness to history in the making…. the second time this first African American chairman of the board of education who performed his duties!!

As we waited to line up and march in I looked to my left and saw four women with locks! Three were facing me and one had her back to me. I knew I could not miss the opportunity to speak to these sisters. Not only did they stand out because they were Sisters of the Diaspora. They stood out because of their multigenerational locked heads. I drifted over to say hello. As I approach the women with her back towards me turned. That woman was Michelle!!!! We had reconnected! By the way…those other beautiful strong sisters where her mother and aunts! How cool is that!!

Michelle has been wearing her hair natural for 4 years. And has been locking for that length of time. Like many she felt the process of locking to be a social one. Her decision connected to a desire to look inward.

"I felt that it would help me to get more in touch with my real self. I wanted to get closer to myself, my real self spiritually, emotionally and physically. She goes on to explain. "My relationship with my hair is like many of my relationships with people. That is, I love my hair, I am proud of it, and I enjoy it. But sometimes I get frustrated with it, tired of it, or overwhelmed by it. But if I just hang in there, it passes and the relationship continues to grow."

Prior to allowing her hair "be" natural she felt that she loved it at that time as well. It seemed to be a love based on conditions.

"I began to not like the idea of hiding or covering up my hair with chemical relaxers. At that time, I did not care too much for my "naps" that would appear after a couple of months as the relaxer grew out. By contrast, since leaving my hair natural, I have discovered that my natural hair is gorgeous. It had curls and waves and twist and turns and naps that I just love. I hadn't even started enjoying letting the naps just hang out rather than trying to meticulously tame them like I used to do. There is a free airy-ness that I like when some of my curly naps are sticking out around my face on their own. Maybe those naps make me feel like a little adventurous girl again?"

Michelle explained that people of European descent often ask questions about her hair. "If I had a dollar for every time someone asked me about or commented on my hair, I would be rich! Most of their (European descent) comments are "I like your hair". Occasionally they may ask me whether it's permanent or temporary, how long it takes to do, etc.

According to Michelle both African-American & European-Americans seem to be troubled by the permanent aspect of locks.

"African-American youth in particular seem overwhelmed by the notion that I would have to cut the locks out and start over in order to go back to other hairstyles. The notion of having to "lose" or cut ones hair seems very worrisome to the teens that ask me about my hair.

"I know we have a thing about hair length in our culture. Hair is our strength, our beauty culturally speaking. Long hair is the thing that many of us wished for while growing up. I think this is due to the European notions of beauty that is promoted through the media. So, to see long locks like I have grown, and to think that one would have to cut them in order in order to change them, well, that's a very scary notion to many of our folks.

When I really think about it, I think that I too am hung up on that notion, but I am working on it. I think that I worry about my attractiveness with very short hair compared to long hair, be it braids or locks."

"Part of my journey right now, is to stop worrying about attractiveness and to appreciate my natural beauty no matter what hairstyle, hair texture, hair length, clothes, make-up, weight or height…But…. To just love me for me.

"Just love me for me"…. wow if only that message was one that was given to our girls by everyone.

Michelle shared with me a story regarding her niece.

"My two nieces were spending time with me this past summer. I enrolled them both in a summer camp focused on multicultural issues and diversity. The camp turned out to be predominantly white in both clientele and staff. In fact, I don't think there was any staff of color. What transpired made me so angry hat I thought I was going to pass out.

Well, one of their teachers, a white male, was horsing around with the kids about a week before camp was to end. One thing lead to another, and the next thing you know, this fool has taken some scissors and is "pretending" to threaten to cut off some of the braids of my niece's hair. She had her hair braided so pretty with beautiful beads and everything. And this idiot had some scissors "pretending" to cut her hair off. In acting this out, he then "accidentally" cuts off a small bit of her hair (a few strands of baby-hair) from near her hairline. And then he proceeds to show her the hair.

She was livid! She freaked out right there in the class and basically told him off and even toppled over some supplies and things (good for her!!). Oh Lord!, When they got home, she didn't want to tell me about it because she knew I would be upset. So, it took my other niece to tell me."

" When I found out I was seeing stars. I immediately got the director of the camp on the phone, and told her what I thought about this. I told her this was a courtesy call because I knew her from various works we had done together in the community. I indicated if I didn't know her I would have called he Department of Children & Families (DCF) first." Michelle made it clear that she had an expectation that the situation would be dealt with immediately and that her next phone call would be to DCF.

"I told her I wanted to know why he had picked the only child in the class and with ethnic braided hairstyle to put in danger with scissors and violate her person by cutting her hair!! The director arranged for a meeting with the teacher, herself and me for the first thing that next morning.

It was a very productive meeting. Of course the teacher apologized up and down. He even cried! He tried to assure me that he had no malicious or racist intentions, and that it would never happen again. I told him to tell that to my nieces and let's see what they think about it!

I explained to him that as a white male, he has the luxury of just going through life without having to carry the history and burden of past abuse and exploitation. That me and my nieces have to remember, in a society that is both racist and sexist. I continued with, that for him, he was just horsing around with some kiddy scissors. But for us, it was an adult against a child; a white man against a black child; a white male adult against a black female child; a white male with a potentially dangerous weapon, kiddy scissors or not, they can still poke someone's eyes out; a white male humiliating and violating their personal space and safety of the only child of color in the class with an ethnic hair style.

Michelle continued by strongly suggesting that he educate himself further on multicultural issues or he would soon find himself facing the possibility of a suit. "I appreciated the fact that he was so apologetic and willing to listen or I might have been the one to sue him and the program.

Her niece's received heartfelt apologies from the teacher and the director. They assured them that they would not be in any of this teacher' classes and would never have to come in contact with him. Michelle left the decision about remaining in the camp to the girls. They decided to forfeit that day and maybe try again the following week. Before leaving to spend that day with her nieces Michelle insisted, "Each of them call the girls parents and discuss the situation with them." "I explained that I and they would have to answer to these girls' parents. And they did. By the following Monday, her nieces were ready to go back and finish the last week of camp, and they did so safely and successfully!

Conversely, Michelle shared the special bonding that has occurred between she and her 14 year old son. Early on in the locking process she offered her son the opportunity to make some money by helping to groom her hair. His response...."he wanted no part of them...he felt locks were ugly, yucky etc."

"Well recently, four years later, I made the offer again. Maybe he was a little uptight for the cash ($30 for him, as opposed to the $90 that a hairdresser would charge if I ever were to have the luxury of going to them.) He said yes to the $30 and I washed my hair. He sat in a chair while I sat on the floor between his legs like folks used to do in the old days. I did some work on my laptop and he and I just rapped with each other about various things. He meticulously twisted each lock. He did such a good job that I gave him a $5 tip! At his request, we penciled in my next 'appointment". It was a wonderful, relaxing, opportunity for quality time between my child and myself. I think he took pride in the job and gleamed when others complimented my hair. I think he also gained a greater appreciation for the feel and texture of my coarse hair. I noticed him putting some of the same gel in his hair that I use. He even seemed to have a greater appreciation for his own coarse curls and waves.

That quality time with him while getting my hair done was one of the most pleasant times I have ever had with my hair.

Tyrone's Journey
"My Hair and I are in Love!"

Tyrone is in his mid-thirties and has had his hair natural for 7 years. He decided seven years ago to lock but only recently has he actually started the locking process. Here is his response when I asked him about his locks.

""I wanted to try something new. I was tried of the so-called conservative look. I felt like a clone…looking like every black businessman at work"

I found this to be an interesting statement. It caused me to think a little about what it takes for a black man to be accepted in the workplace. Certainly locks were not going to add to a black mans acceptability, Particularly in the white business arena.

To be accepted, there is a need to adopt a certain way of dressing, speaking and behaving. If one is out of step with what is "acceptable" it is difficult to move ahead. A black man who decides to go outside of the norm of acceptable hair (i.e. close-cropped, neat and conservative) is definitely taking a risk.

As a male, Tyrone explained that the transition was somewhat different than that a female may encounter. "I never really struggled with the issue of my hair. I know that a lot of women do. Since making the decision to lock all I can say is my hair and I are in love."

"It is interesting how others have responded to my locking. My family and friends could not believe it. I had been in the church most of my life and had adopted what I thought was a way of looking as a church going man. You know stepping outside the norm in my church sends a message that you must be a homosexual!. Amazingly, I used to think that way. Obviously I don't feel that way anymore. Now I know your hair has nothing to do with your sexual orientation.

I have come to like this lock look on myself and so do most others. Occasionally I run into people, white, black whoever who don't like it. But I just deal with it. I have even put up with the stares and rejection from employers who have not wanted to hire me because of my hair. I just deal with it!"

Trula's Journey

"Yes, its all my hair, and NO you may NOT touch my locks!"

"Would you look at that...I wonder if it's all hers...Oh my god, they're so shiny...

Only when I heard, "I'm going to ask if I can touch them" did I realize they were talking about me? Pulling myself out of daydreaming, I quickly turned to face the other passengers in the elevator I was riding in. "Yes, its all my air and no, you may NOT touch my locks!" when the elevator door arrived at the next floor as I got off I gave them a show. I shook my locks out and flung them over my shoulder. TAKE THAT!!

My locks often awe people, and I get asked a lot of questions about them. The primary question is, of course, why did you lock your hair?

The main reason I locked my hair is because I have always liked and admired locks on other people. I can remember being four years old and seeing a woman with locks down to her knees and being totally awed by her hair. I knew that I wanted to have hair like that when I grew up.

I am lucky in that both my parents are proud of being black and they taught that to me and my sisters and brothers. I have mostly worn my hair in natural styles most of my life and thus I have thick, healthy hair. I know that a lot of people don't have this background so their way to dreads is fraught with drama and complications. Although I didn't experience it, I understand the emotional battle they had to go through to get to the point of being proud of their natural hair.

My journey to locks started as mere vanity, i.e. I liked the way they looked and knew they would look cute on me. Along the way I learned about locks, their history, and how to care for them. It has been a wonderful journey and an uplifting experience."[4]

---

[4] Breckenridge, Trula, Dread Mama website 2001

Sandy's Journey

"I will never straighten my hair again"

"Over a year has passed and I am well along in my journey. I can't tell you how happy I am with my nappily happily locked hair. During this journey I have met some of the most wonderful people.... many of whom I hope to keep as friends for life...some of whom I'll probably lose track of along the way. But there is one thing I can say with an absolute certainty I will never again straighten my hair!

In the early months of 2000 I decided to stop frying my hair with relaxers and chemicals. I finally realized that since God didn't give me straight hair, I should stop my misguided and futile attempts to improve on perfection. I'd wanted to stop relaxing my hair for a long time, but I DID'NT KNOW WHAT ON EARTH TO DO WITH THIS HEAD FULL OF STEEL WOOL that I was born with. I do have to go to work every day after all, and I don't want to scare my co-workers with hair out to there.

During my search for the perfect natural style, I discovered there is a movement towards natural hair in the black community; but most cosmetologists aren't embracing this movement at all, for fear that it will cut into their incomes. Therefore, it's not easy to find good-looking styles or competent stylists for natural African-American hair. I didn't think dreads are for me, and I didn't want to look like I just stuck my finger into an electric socket, which is pretty much what my natural hair looks like.

Finally, I stumbled upon a relatively new locking technique for natural highly textured (nappy) hair. It is called Sisterlocks®. It doesn't have to be taken down or redone constantly. The hair grows; it can be cut, set styled, etc. Just what I wanted! And I never have to be afraid of sweat, fog, humidity, or rain reverting my hair to its natural state again, because it's already natural! Yeah! I decided this was the one for me!

I started this site (website) on June 17 2000 as I was in the process of growing out at least two inches of new (kinky) roots. Two inches gave me enough new growth to get my Sisterlocks®. I found a wonderful Sisterlocks® consultant right here in Detroit at Everette's Corn-Row & Braiding Academy, and she took me across and has helped me along the way. I couldn't wait for my appointment on July 21st! Believe me, the decision to go from that artificial chemically straightened look to any kind of natural style is a big one, and I needed all the help I could get to help me through the transition! I found some wonderful email groups that have been so helpful in this regard.

Valencia's Journey

"Locking is not a trend...It is a Life Change"

Valencia (Lynn) is a friend but in reality she is a family member. You know the kind of person that when you first meet, you are sure your paths are destined to stay crossed, connected and together forever!

I met Lynn in Undergrad way back in 1972!! We lived in the same dorm. We have been through some stuff!! In college we were into the wig thing. On Friday or Saturday night we would get hooked –up. Dressed to the nines, platforms, shiny satin, wigs and all. You couldn't tell us we weren't fine!! As the years passed our taste in clothes, shoes and hair have changed. We are both in our mid and late forties respectively. And although we might not consider the highest heals or the tightest pants as appropriate attire now, we still love looking good.

We would often compare our hair. I felt my hair was way too thin; Lynn was always been concerned about her baby fine hair and the bald spots at her temples. Through the years we have occasionally taken a parallel course with our hair. Like when she learned how to braid extensions and taught me. I continued to braid my hair and Lynn too several other routes.

In June 2001, during an interview for this book Lynn still had her hair in a weave. She had been contemplating the Lock Thing, since just prior to the Nappy & Happy conference that April.

"I had a Jerhi curl and got tired of it so I went back to weaving it and letting my hair go natural in anticipation of going on the lock journey. I have always had an ambivalent and stressful relationship with my hair because of the bald spots at my temples. Finding complimentary styles has been difficult. I couldn't even wear my dream style of a ponytail because of the bald spots. I first started wearing braids over 20 years ago, it was the first time I felt empowered and free. I have come to the conclusion that I locking will lead me back to that feeling.

I started to see locks as the norm. I was feeling self-conscious and a little pressure about not being locked. I wanted to be a part of the Community. People close to me were locking and I began to realize that locking was not a trend; it is a life change."

Lynn started to lock 2 months ago!! So did her daughter. "I took the weave out and started. I don't know about this, but I am doing it. I keep a wig on over it while at work. I am not ready to let them show and I know the people at work aren't ready to see them!" I assured her that there will come a point were she'll take the wig off and it will all be good!!

Joi's Journey
"I am finally free"

Joi is a 21-year-old college student. She has been wearing her hair in an Afro for four months. " I realized I didn't even know what my hair looked like without color, thermal straightening and chemical straightening. I wanted to know what I was changing and what I was missing.

Having my hair natural has made me feel more connected and in touch with my identity as a black women. I am still learning about my hair and learning to accept it in its natural state, but my hair is showing its love for me now that I've freed it from the oppression of the perm.

Before going natural, my hair filled me with conceit and a false sense of pride. I thought I was "Loving" my hair, but all I was really doing was fooling myself. All the extra work and time I spent on my hair only added to my false sense of who I was."

When I decided to have my hair cut my mother was against it at first. She called the salon five times to get the stylist to stop. I felt hurt, humiliated and embarrassed that day. A day I wanted to feel special and symbolic. My mother still isn't thrilled with the way my hair looks, but every now and again she pays me a compliment. My father and grandfather have been perfectly nice about it. My friends and other people of color have been supportive, although occasionally someone will say "why did you do that to your self! Caucasian folks have told me how "adorable" I am with a "fro" or "Curls"…(those are the words they use to describe my hair."

The decision to go natural has created a sense of pride and connectedness for Joi. "I can wash it and go! I can wear it curly! I can wear it in an Afro! I can go swimming! I can workout and let myself sweat! I AM FINALLY FREE! I don't have to limit myself or live around my hair. People of all ages compliment me on my hair and tell me how beautiful I look. I am learning to accept myself in my natural state and growing to love the way I look.

AND ALL OF THIS CAME ABOUT FROM A SINGLE, SIMPLE HAIR CUT!!

Kelley's Journey

"I have a reminder scar on my neck that acts as my Sankofa"

"I had shoulder length hair and was curling it one day. I dropped the curlers and burned my neck. I made up my mind to free myself that day. I have a reminder scar on my neck that acts as my Sankofa.

I really didn't have a bad relationship with my hair, it has always been pretty cooperative and I was always changing things up. I think the friction came when my hair experienced freedom and rebirth and I tried to go back to bondage. That was short lived.

I have been wearing my hair in locks for 6 years. As a result my relationship with my hair is definitely improving, as we grow closer together. There are times when I think we both drive each other crazy. I am learning however, to allow my hair to be what it needs to be and in turn, I become who I'm supposed to be!

My immediate family really liked my natural hair. My father loved the simple natural look. He said it showed off my face. My husband, however, was a little concerned that I might look a little masculine. (He was a lover of long, curly flowing locks) He has grown, however, to really like it and now that my locks have some length, he can once again, enjoy "long, curly flowing locks".

My extended family members were not fond of my natural hair or locks. They wondered what I was doing with it and when I was going to grow out of this stage. (especially, my southern family members). Later their sentiments changed to "I wish I had the guts to do that".

Surprisingly people of European descent have responded very positively to my hair. They are very curious and sometimes want to touch and even try it on their hair. I get compliments from my Euro "liberal" classmates to my Euro "conservative" elderly patients that I take care of especially elderly, white men!

Sam's Journey

"It's a Spiritual Thing"

Growing up, Sam was often teased about his dark skin, big nose and nappy hair. African features.... strong features that speak of the motherland...features that connect you to who we all are.

Sam is a soft-spoken, spirit filled man of 48 who recently started to lock his hair. We met at the first Nappy & Happy conference I developed and offered. He wanted to video the event for a local cable network show he was producing. Since then we keep in touch often sharing the experience of locking.

As a man who is well known in his western Massachusetts town his decision to lock created some interesting responses. "I am a politician, entrepreneur, and a Christian. I truly feel that locking is a Spiritual thing. When I first went to my church with my new twist one of the elders at the church said something like...you are a role model, when I see you again I don't want to see those things in your hair! Amazing.... many older people see locks as something distasteful.

The truly amazing thing is since I started to lock I have found a certain silence within myself. I don't have to talk. There is a power and sensuality that I have connected with and others seem to connect to as well. I feel more culturally grounded. I am clear that this is not a hairstyle but a reality. It IS and IS!

Our hair is a gift that we have been given by GOD. The process Locking is being manifested within this gift!"

Anita's Journey

"My hair needed a rest and so did my brain!"

Anita has been wearing her hair in braid extensions for 2 years. "I decided to let my hair be natural for its health. There is certain ease to wearing braids, a freedom. I realized that the freedom braids provided was not only for my hair but also for my brain. My brain was feeling liberated and confident.

I was losing my hair because of the perm. I can say I felt a release once I decided to let the perm grow out. My hair needed a rest and so did my brain.

I do recall one very painful thing that happened as a result of this positive change for my hair and me. A friend of my mother's said if my mom were alive she would kill me if she saw my hair…. That hurt!

Karen's Journey

"I feel my hair is another expression of self"

Talent comes in many forms. All of us have some; most of us are unaware of what ours might be. Karen is not one of those people. Her art is distinctive and speaks of a new generation of black female artist. I love her work and love her spirit even more.

"I have had my hair natural for four years. At that time I wore it in a very close cut. I had decided to go natural to be spiritually sound."

Prior to going natural Karen states, "My relationship with my hair was one were I was keeping up with the Jones. I received compliments on my hair when it was processed. I dreaded having to get a relaxer.... especially if I sat too long. I've always been one to take care of my hair on a weekly basis...perms...relaxers...close-cropped. Why go through the pain...I've always liked me. My locks make me like me even more. One thing is for sure...I will never go back to being processed again. If I were to change I'd go back to my "boyish haircut". It definitely was against the norm...but so are locks. Different Works!"

Karen had been locking 4 months when I first met her in September. She was the featured artist at a gallery open house the week after September 11th 2001. There were a lot of Nappy and Happy sisters around. We had some deep conversations that afternoon about messages, destiny, and our hair.

Karen shared " I feel my hair is another expression of self. Being an artist...I've always been a free spirit watching my locks so their own thing is a creative process, taking place on my head. Each lock does its own thing...It reminds me of me!

My family likes my hair. My sister has locks...She is happy I'm nappy. My mom is just glad to see me with hair again. My friends have basically paid me complements. White folks on the street unfortunately clutch their pocketbooks...White folks in the art world view me as an extension of my work. It's just kind of deep how people look at my hair before they look into my eyes.

The most painful story I can remember having to do with my hair was when I was a pre-teen. I never had "good-hair" as they called it. So the kids at school teased me about it. That messed with my self-esteem. Then as I grew I realized GOD reach down and gave me a gift of my own. A gift to create with my hands and my head.... I no longer give a damn what any one thinks about my hair.

Since I have begun to lock, when I am driving I turn my rear view mirror to look at my hair instead of it being pointed in the direction of my back window...This happens no matter whose car I drive.... Deep huh...?

Andrea's Journey
"Can't you save it??!!"

One day while searching the web for sites on natural hair I came across Kinks R Us©. What a great find!! I immediately emailed the creator of the site. We had several email conversations about natural hair and the conference I was planning (Nappy & Happy). Andrea agreed to be a speaker at the conference. What a delight she was!! She has this incredible smile and infectious laugh. She had never done any public speaking and was surprised at the audience positive response to her nappy story.

"There are a few reasons why I decided to start my site. Not just because I'd toyed with the idea of creating my own website for a rather long time. Not just because I felt us females needed more information and support when making the big decision to "Go Natural" and not just because creating a website of my very own was one of my homework assignments...But because, it was Just Time!

I'm not quite sure why I made the sudden decision to stop punishing my hair, but I remember very well what lead up to it.

The summer of '98 was good to me I was visiting the hairdresser every 9 weeks for the 4 hour-long Optimum Relaxer hair session. With snacks, newspaper and cell phone stuffed neatly in my bag, I was prepared to spend as long as necessary waiting for my favorite beautician to get around to getting rid of my nasty embarrassing nappy roots. Hey, I might even go out to the club tonight. I'd have a fresh, shiny, just come out of the beauty salon looking straight head of hair.

Because my hair was growing like wild it was time to ruin it, I had to have color; it had to be red. I wasn't gonna pay at least $60 for my favorite hairdresser to put the color on for me, Yeah, I liked her but not that much! I'd messed with my hair before, it hadn't always been successful, but this time, this time would be different. I mean, how wrong could you go with a semi-permanent color?

The first application of red was not quite red enough, maybe it did look red when I went out into the summer sun, but hey, why patch up, I wanted everybody to see that brilliant red, even when dark, just like in the magazines. So the following week I colored it again, and left the red on for one hour. I threw a plastic cap on for good measure, you know so the color would really take. Well, the only thing it really took was my hair!

I ran to my favorite hairdresser almost in tears. "Cut it", she said, "can't you save it? " I argued, "well we could try" she said unconvincingly. So I spent double my usual amount and got a deep treatment, just as she recommended. I was desperate.

During the next few weeks I was still losing hair left, right and center. Braids, I thought.. That always works. After 4 months of sporting braids the damage had long been done. I had to come to terms with the fact that I had ruined my hair and the bad hair had to go.

In January '99 I made the appointment, packed my snacks, newspaper and cell phone neatly in my bag and with sunken shoulders and head down, I eased into her chair. I felt like Sampson, all my strength cut clean away as my favorite hairdresser cut my hair down to 1 inch. I was left with a plastered down style/look kinda thing (I had to beg for 2 inches to be left at the front). My favorite hairdresser made an appointment for me to come back in another month for another serious double the price treatment.

As the date drew nearer I grew tried. Tried of the "haircapades", tried of the trials and tribulations, tried of 21 years of relaxer, wet look, another relaxer, a jheri curl, then a product that promised you could go curly to straight to back to curly all within 1 hour, a relaxer, another jheri curl that "didn't take" which I had to go through embarrassingly for 4 months, then back to a relaxer. Bear in mind, in between all this hair torture I was braiding and putting in a weave in here and there."

These processes created a love hate relationship between Andrea and her hair. Now she states she has "nothing but love for my hair."

Andrea has decided to lock. For sometime she debated beginning that journey because of its permanence. Her sister is joining her in the lock journey.

Donna's Journey
"My hair is nappy and I aint mad"

Martha's Vineyard is a vacation Mecca for many African-Americans. It is a place were you could see grandmothers, great-grandfathers, daughters, sons, nieces, Dad's, nanas and aunts connecting, reflecting and having a good time. We have vacationed there for 10 years.

Last summer while vacationing at the "Inkwell", soaking up some rays and watching the array of beautiful black folk, I noticed a beautiful sister with her hair in twists. I asked her if she would be interested in taking part in this book. She agreed. Here is her story.

Donna is a 32 year old, from New Jersey. She has not had a perm (or any other chemical in her hair since June 23, 1995. Occasionally she may straighten it (hot comb) or get braids.

"I decided I didn't like the way the relaxer had changed the texture of my hair. There was also the piece of me that is difficult to explain, but I actually felt kind of angry that I had to get a perm. I was like, why do I have to have my hair straight? It's not the natural way my hair grows out of my head so why do I have to subject myself to a burning scalp, hours in the salon and everything else. The answer…just because that is what you're "expected" or "supposed" to do.

Before I decided to get rid of the perm I was looking at other peoples' hair all the time. I became fascinated with the different natural textures of African-American hair. I didn't know what the natural texture of my hair would be like but I decided to do it. I just let my perm grow out and I started to trimming the ends (I decided that I didn't want to cut my hair short.). It was a difficult process because my permed hair and my natural hair did not have a smooth meeting!

I had liked my hair when I had a relaxer. But I didn't like that I had to put chemicals in my hair to get it that way and I felt that I was damaging my hair. I was able to wear it in various ways, but the expense and time factors to get it the way I wanted were much more when my hair was permed. Now, except when I get braids I do my hair myself.

The relationship I have with my hair now is positive although I must say that I can't say that I would never go back to having a perm. Doing my hair takes a lot of work because I have so much hair. But when I am done doing whatever …I really like it. I even had a dream one time that I had gotten a perm and I was really sad until I woke up and found out that it was a dream!

I like the natural texture of my hair, especially when I wear it in twists. I often think that if my hair were a lot shorter the amount of work I have to do to get it done would not be a factor. I also get a lot of compliments on my hair. I enjoy wearing my hair in many different ways and being natural is conducive to that.

It is interesting how people react to my natural hair. Now that natural hair is becoming much more popular (acceptable) I receive a lot of positive feedback regarding my hair. When I first decided to go natural I know my hair must have looked crazy at times because it was half straight and half natural. My mother expressed some concern about why I was doing it. Actually, at the time I had recently joined a church and she tried to make a connection to my decision to go natural with the church I had joined. Even now I look back on that and I laugh. My mother has one of those cold curly perms and she ascribes to the same mindset of many black women, which is if your hair is not permed, it is not done.

Many of my friends who have relaxers say to me "I have to have a perm", like its something they can't live without. That, I don't laugh at because I think we've been so brainwashed in this country to believe that our natural hair is just not good enough; we have to do something with this "mess" that grows out of our head in order for it to be right, done, or acceptable to ourselves and to others.

Some of my friends say they like my hair but say they could never do it. But because my hair was very long before I went natural I know some of them wonder why I did it. Like they think I had nice hair before so why would I go and ruin it.

As far as comments from non-blacks, I've received a lot of compliments. The slightest thing usually fascinates them. If I wear my hair differently three days in a row they are amazed. When I wear twists they wonder how long it took me to do, how do I get it to stay" like that" they want to touch it etc. When I take the twist out and just let it go wild it's amazing the attention I get from guys who are non-black! I think they think I am wilder than my hair!

I even try to watch what I say about my hair. Even though I don't have children (yet) I don't want to make them feel negatively about their hair by saying stupid stuff like "bad hair vs. good hair" or calling their hair "mess".

It is painful to think we (African-Americans) are made to feel bad about our natural hair. Still something in us is triggered when we see a woman with an Afro, be it very closely cut or not. We think something is wrong with it, it's not nice, or somehow maybe its OK on her because she can "pull it off"…meaning she may have a natural hair style but somehow her nice face or the nice shape of her head makes up for the fact that she's really sporting a nappy head!

Donna ended her sharing with me by offering this poem.

My hair is nappy and I aint mad
Though you may see me and shake your head
To me, what I've got isn't bad
My natural hair is not a fad
Its just the way that my hair grows
And so I let it
Now you know
That I'm just trying to be me
Whether fizzy, curly or kinky
These tresses stresses to be free!

Carolyn's Journey
"Better than ever"

I met Carolyn (a good friend of Valencia's) at my book signing in 1999. I noticed her right a way. I was standing on the opposite side of the room as she entered. There she stood with her locks and a "funky" little head wrap. Oh how I wanted to lock! As I was introduced to her I couldn't help but say, 'I really want to lock but I'm not sure. I am not even sure of the exact words she used, but what ever they were her voice was so calming, serene and spiritual. I felt immediate acceptance and support.

Carolyn has had her hair natural for about 12 years often wearing goddess and micro-braids. She has been locked for 5 of those years. She said, "beauty parlors weren't gettin it and my relationship with my hair was one of hard work to make it look "good". I got tired...then I realized the beauty of natural hair. Now my relationship with my hair is better than ever!

My first year of locking was rough.... (and it shouldn't have been) I would look at other peoples locks and think...I want yours. After about 9 months "I got it! The "ugly stage" was over. For those months my hair grew very slowly. When I "got it" my hair started growing like crazy and it continues to.

I had been natural for so long, my Family was not surprised about my locking. However none of them would have done it then. Now there are a couple of my relatives who have. My mother is even considering it! What is important about locking is you never anticipate the spiritual connection. That spiritual connection tells me I'm growing spiritually.

Carolyn attends a church were 70% of the parishioners are locked!!

Gloria's Journey
"Opening my hair and my antennae"

Gloria has had her hair in locks for 3 years. We have been friends for about 4 years. She is one of those people GOD put in my path and that path has grown. The vision of her locks that day we met for lunch moved me to take that lock wig off my head. She was indeed a catalyst for my accepting my locks, being ok with the process and journey to come.

We have since had numerous lunches, phone calls, visit and conversations about our locks. We often find our selves touching one another's hair and saying... "Girl they look good"..."Don't you just love your hair were"...isn't it just great to get up and go!! We laugh hug and wonder aloud how we can get others to join the affirming community of locked heads.

On one occasion Gloria shared her journey.

" I had a natural (short "fro") and was interested in letting it grow and "be". I began to learn about locking, trying to decide if locking is for me. I now realize it was a life changing decision, an experience of which I am "loving". The process of locking speaks to me. It has kept me still...opening my hair and my antennae.

Prior to this decision I did not have a positive relationship with my hair in its natural state. Nappy was bad, so I had to change the natural state to feel ok...you know straight and lying down!

Generally people have responded positively to my locks. What I find interesting is the fact that there are people of European descent who are locking. I guess it is an anti-establishment thing. Although I wonder why is it that they want to imitate us if we are so awful. I feel the imitating says they KNOW OUR GREATNESS!

Linda's Journey

"I wanted to be ME, therefore I decided my hair had to BE!"

Linda is a sister-friend of Gloria's. Over the last couple of years we have connected as a group of nappy sisters who occasionally meet to eat, drink, smile, laugh and support one another. When I first met Linda she wasn't sure about locking. She was indeed letting her hair "BE". It was a mass of thick and curly hair that said, Hello I am here. Her hair has been natural for 5 years. Finally a little over a year ago she decided to lock.

"I wanted to be me, therefore I decided my hair had to be". Prior to going natural I didn't have a relationship with my hair. I fixed or had my hair fixed and struggled with attempting to make my hair look good.

From childhood I remember the pain, agony and work involved in maintaining the "done" look. I use to get so many burns on my ears and neck from the straightening comb. I can still feel the burns and still smell my hair burning! I remember the rationale I was given was, if you wanted to be beautiful there had to be a little pain! I can remember protesting silently (cause back then a child could not voice disagreement) that it shouldn't hurt to be beautiful.

My family has been amazed at my decision to be natural and to lock. Friends have been mixed in their response. Some are supportive others are skeptical. They wonder, what does it mean, why am doing it and what is it that I am going through that would make me do this to my hair?

Other people of color love it, are doing it themselves or want to do it. Occasionally, one might make a comment alluding to, I must be militant or better yet…"I am biting of my nose to spite my face". Meaning I am narrowing opportunities for my self.

People of European descent are mixed in their reactions. They are, stunned, bewildered or amazed. One asked me…"what is that in your hair… oh…you have a shell in your hair!" Or I'll get the preverbal, what if you change your mind question. They don't understand that this decision to lock is the result of my listening to myself. I feel more focused about what I will and will not tolerate.

Carla's Journey

"I don't have a bad hair day!"

Carla lives in New York. New York is definitely the lock Mecca of the United States. She has been locking her hair since 1993. Her decision to lock was a culturally conscious one.

" I can remember being at a street festival in Brooklyn. There was nothing but some people with locks. I felt like I didn't belong. Soon I was thinking about locking my hair.

My boyfriend at the time was very negative about the idea. I thought about it a lot …got rid of him and started to lock! (Funny thing is he is now locked!)

I look back and realize it has been a long road getting to this wonderful relationship I now have with my hair. I have had perms, gone to the hairdresser every 2 weeks, washes, curls, worried about the window being down and the wind blowing holes in my hair…. everything. I even figured out how to sleep and get up with my hair still looking freshly done!

Now I have this freedom! I have encouraged family and friends to lock.

Kathy T's Journey
"Natural hair is weather proof!"

Kathy attended the Nappy and Happy Conference I organized.

She was inspired and felt a real sense of belonging. She agreed to participate in an interview session regarding the book. What follows are a combination of her comments and her responses to a questionnaire.

" I have had my hair natural on and off for 7 years. For the past 2 years I have been solidly natural. In graduate school, I had very little financial means. I was so broke; I was eating fast food discount menus. I hate fast food.

Nevertheless, I realized I could save time and money by going natural. After several mishaps with home relaxers and not being able to find a good beautician when I relocated to Ohio, it made a lot of sense to go close-cropped. I also felt free.

My relationship with my hair in the past was simply unhealthy. When a relaxer was put into my hair at 12 years old, I became unhealthy and developed low self-esteem. Because the African-American community I lived in saw such (a relaxer) as a rite of passage for young girls.

For me, it was a profound realization that my value in the community wad focused on my hair and not my intellect, my make –up and not my reasoning skills, my perfume and clothes instead of my dreams.

Now…simply speaking, I've disregarded the external (relaxers, fakeness) for the authentic (natural hair). I feel great. The challenge is still taking care of my hair. When I have to style it, I'm challenged. So, I'm going to start to lock. Locking fits my lifestyle.

There is an old Chinese proverb that says "State your position and others will adjust accordingly" The same can be said about my attitude with my hair. My family has had mixed reactions regarding my decision. The short cropped look frightened them. One time my father teasingly called me a boy. When my hair was longer and naturally wild, an African-American female supervisor stated, " We have to do something about your hair". She gave me the name of her beautician. I ignored her and got braids.

On one occasion some of my African-American co-workers became angry with me when I did not agree with them on an issue, which would have negatively impacted black students. One of them wrote "Nappy"(in reference to me) all over my office and building. It wasn't painful for me…. but I pained for them, for their complete lack of pride. The funny thing is people of European descent have only positive comments about my hair. Many wonder why we use relaxers when our natural hair is beautiful.

Natural hair is weather proof! It is exhilarating. Before, with relaxers I could <u>not</u> fully enjoy the rain, swim in the ocean, hike or even enjoy gardening without worrying about my relaxed style "sweating out".

Now, I'm free and my natural hair seems to thrive in the sun like an okra plant which grows tall and strong. My hair likes its leaves and flowers bask in the sun. Relaxed hair bakes in the sun, my natural hair basks and thrives in the sun!

Teresa's Journey

"Who would have imagined that hair could cause so much drama?"

My Dilemma

"I didn't plan for this to be an introspective experience, but that's what it has turned out to be. Really this kicked off my whole self-discovery journey. Who would have imagined that hair could cause so much drama? How can hair be political? Let me take you on a journey of still un-chartered proportions…the final frontier…Are you excited? What I'm trying to say is that I am still on this journey so stay tuned for updates and so forth.

Anyway, in the winter of 1998, my dermatologist instructed me to never put another harsh chemical in my hair or on my scalp. I had been having chronic skin and scalp irritations and my hair had been falling out from the root for almost a year. I could also tell the texture of my hair had changed. Because I have aunts and cousins who developed Alopecia in their 30's, I was terrified that this is what was happening to me, so I went to a dermatologist. She took several cultures and gave me antibiotics and prescriptions for my skin and told me to come back in 3 months.

I needed a touch up badly but I could not put any chemicals in my hair until after I went back for my follow-up appointment, or so I thought. During this time, I wore a wig. I got nothing but compliments and my co-workers affectionately called me "Tina Turner". MY wearing mini skirts and leather boots probably helped the image too. Well I've certainly been called worse!! It was funny…although I felt attractive and got plenty of compliments from people, I felt like I was trying to front. Like everyone knew I was wearing a wig and, after I turned my back, talked about me saying I was trying to "fool somebody". I know it was all in my head because many people said they would have never known I was wearing a wig if I hadn't told them. Regardless, it wasn't me. Oh, and don't let a strong wind blow by…I was praying that I didn't lose my hair in public! On the outside, I was "Fly" but on the inside, I was very insecure.

The Braids

When I went back to the dermatologist, I was told my hair loss and everything must have been due to stress because I did not have Alopecia, but I did have Psoriasis. She told me to never put anymore-harsh chemicals in my hair and to just wear it natural. I told her there was "no way in hell" that I could go through all the maintenance it would take to maintain my hair naturally and look decent. She couldn't possibly understand, for she had straight hair! She went through the song and dance of how the chemicals were so bad for my hair and so on. I wasn't trying to hear her. I was gonna go to the beauty supply store and buy me a home perm on the way home!!

When she left the room, I asked the nurse if that lady knew what she was talking about. I felt, since the nurse was black, that she would feel a sista and tell me what I wanted to hear. The nurse agreed with the dermatologist 100% and told me I should avoid the chemicals. She then went on to give me the phone number of a girl who braided her hair when she was avoiding chemicals. I found it humorous that this particular nurse was sporting a bone straight perm at the time. Anyway I went home…by-passed the beauty supply store and contemplated my situation.

How could something as insignificant as hair give me so much stress? I decided to try the braids for a while. I wore braids for 8 months. I just knew I was fine, Nubian sista. I had the open-ended braids with Kanekalon®, I had human hair (which really sucked) and I had the full individuals. No one ever braided my hair for less than $150 and in less than 8.5 hours. I hated spending 15 hours just to take the braids out, only to turn around and spend another whole day, sitting up in someone's house or braid shop just to be "beautiful". I hated sitting there; not knowing what the hell was being said while the braiders spoke a different language all the time I was there, unless they were talking to me. I hated having to tell the braider to ease up as tears welled-up in my eyes from the pulling and tugging. I hated having to pay someone damn near $50 to watch my kids all day while I went to get "beautiful". I hated when my butt went to sleep from having to sit in the chair or on that pillow too long. The last time I had my hair braided, I lost 5 whole braids because they were done too tightly. I am talking about my hair coming out from the root and looking down at a long braid, lying on the floor!! I had bald spots on my edges and in the back of my head! What the hell was going on?? This was not supposed to be happening!!!

Needless to say, I said "forget it…no more braids". I thought, maybe, I could just wear my hair back in a bun for a while. Maybe even get a hairpiece to stick back there to make it look perfect. Don't you know, I could not, for the life of me, get my hair to lie down? Forget about gels, mousses, styling sprays, grease, oil, tying down...all that stuff! My hair would NOT lie down. I had this poof with something straggly having off the ends. I was sooooo... depressed. I pulled out my wig again. I researched and researched natural hair and of the little I found, I decided to try dreads. I figured, my curl pattern is too tight to get the Lisa Nicole Carson (the actress) look. I wasn't a short Afro kinda sista. I don't think I'm an Afro sista at all actually. Anyway, I searched for a loctitian. Can you believe they were few and far between in Atlanta? I'm talking Atlanta, GA! The black Mecca! What's wrong with THIS picture?

Giving In

I met a few people who specialize in natural hair...or so they claimed. I looked at their books and what I saw was no more than cornrows and braids and something called Nubian twists that looked like crippled worms growing out folks' heads! Not to mention one of the women in the shops (the one doing the most talking), with dreads down her behind, but there was no kinda pattern or anything to it. It was more like a wild Afro...about 3'' long, with hunks of...of...I don't know what. She kept telling me about going through an "ugly stage". I said to myself, "it doesn't look like I'll ever come out of it if I do what you tell me to do". Needless to say, I just picked a lady and crossed my fingers.

I put on my wig and went to Claudia. Claudia two-strand twisted my hair and told me not to cut the perm off the ends because the ends would be blunt and the twist would not stay. When she finished, she turned me around to the mirror and I wanted to cry! The hair itself looked good, but I didn't like the style with my face. I felt doomed and I think I hurt Claudia's feelings because, I immediately said "I'm going to buy me another wig tomorrow". The twists were nice and puffy but the ends, where the perm was, was just stringy. I didn't like that at all. I went home and my 11-year-old son jumped and said, "I thought you had bought someone home with you... I didn't recognize you... Wow, that's real different". My 4-year old daughter said, "Mommy your hair is pretty." I went and looked in the mirror again. I could not believe I walked into a beauty shop and paid $75, spent 5 hours in there and came out looking worse than I did when I went in (with my Tina Turner wig)!! I tried to curl the little twists like some of the micro-braided styles I've seen but the curls would not stay. I decided to get out that weekend and just get a feel for the reactions I would get.

I recall running errands and being so self-conscious, thinking everyone was looking at me and wondering what was up with my hair. The ultimate test, or so I thought, was when I stopped to get gas. There was a group of 5 young guys, standing near where I had parked my car. Now, I have always thought I was somewhat attractive. I usually get at least a devilish glance if not a "hey baby…what 'cho name is and where is yo man?' I walked past the guys and not one glance! You could have thought I was invisible! I was crushed. My spirit was broken. Not only was I invisible now, but I had discovered that I was vain too!! Oh, the agony of it all!!

I went home and cried. My kids thought I was having a nervous breakdown. I kept trying to lift myself up. I purposefully stayed in until the wig shops closed so I had to go to work like this. I kept telling myself that I was being silly. That I am still the great person inside that I've always been. I told myself that now; men who approach me will be doing so because they are truly interested in me not my abilities to "<u>back dat thing up</u>"! I had this internal battle going on with in me.

I had to re-think what I really felt about myself...about beauty...about black hair...about our culture...about the media and misconceptions and self-hatred that I had learned over the years and internalized.

Reality and Awareness

I went to work that morning with a full face of make-up. (Usually I just wear lipstick) I got compliments all day. They loved it! I was thinking to myself, "these folks are either crazy or they are just trying to make me feel better". Believe it or not, the only negative comments came from black folks. One brotha felt the need to tell me that he didn't like it. I never asked for his opinion anyway. A sista told me she like braids better. I began to use that comment the loctician gave me about the "ugly stage". I recall my boss telling me that I am far from ugly and it put a band-aid on my ego for a minute. I was going through turmoil and no one could understand how I felt. I didn't even understand it.

I got on the Internet…I love this place…and began to do more research. I found some forums on natural hair and literally spent about 3 full workdays, reading through archives of forums about natural hair and locs. There were women out there going through the same thing! Some women were even experiencing worse! I was so encouraged by the helpfulness and the bonds that were formed in those forums! I joined a few and although I don't write a lot, I contribute here and there. I've been wanting to set up a website about my experience in hopes that I can further help those experiencing similar situations and help myself to understand my journey. Some days I do, but some I don't.

I've always been one who marches to a different drummer…. a strong-willed woman who does what SHE feels and doesn't try to fit into anyone's mold. I always pride myself on being different from the norm but not so much that I drew attention to myself. I just always liked to be free to do my own thing and if you tried to constrain or control me, I would fight you tooth and nail to break free. I always believed that I could do anything if I put my mind to it and, looking back on my life thus far, I pretty much accomplished everything I've ever put my mind to do! Now, why would a women such as myself, have such a "thing" about hair?

I've come to learn that my hair is my crown and glory. If I'm proud of what GOD blessed me with, then I should be able to look at it and say "beautiful". I have had press 'n curl, perm upon perm, curls upon curls, braids, homemade weaves, wigs, you name it! I don't recall EVER getting a perm and not being burned. I've been burned so badly that my hair stuck to my head and it took over a week to get it unstuck and clear the scabs. These weren't only home perms, but beautician applied perms too! Need I say that all beauticians are not created equal? But, you knew that, right? I've had both my ears and my neck burnt from straightening combs…burnt my forehead with electric curlers….Its just not a pretty journey no matter WHAT I did to my hair. I despise spending a lot of time in beauty salons…never liked that. I had a few bad hair days and pretty much kept myself well groomed, according to society's standards.

Acceptance and Growth

I am about 3 months into my twists. Three weeks ago, I got a bug up my behind and took all my twist out and called myself straightening up the parts. I re-twisted it and was amazed are the length I noticed. I had, over time, cut off the perm and I liked the twists much better without the scraggly parts. I have to wash my hair once a week due to the Psoriasis so that is slowing down my "loc-ing process, I'm sure. When I took my twists down that one time, some were almost loc-ed in the middle. I could kick myself for doing that. Oh well…live and learn

Hairzion's Journey
"This is a salon, not a magic shop"

"It was the summer of 1996, and I was at my wit's end. I had just completed another phase in my endless battle of achieving a hairstyle that would be somewhat carefree. I had just removed the braided extensions from my hair and had about maybe one inch of virgin hair. I thought about replacing the braids, but the thought of sitting through hours of another braided style just wasn't appealing at the time.

I started thinking, and as I reflected back to my childhood, I recounted spending many hours in my grandmother's kitchen waiting to get my hair straightened. I pictured myself sitting there, seeing the steel comb on the stove. Usually, I'd be very excited because no matter how unpleasant the process I was about to endure, the end result for me would be manageable, straight hair. So, there I sat, with a towel wrapped tightly around my neck, holding my ears and squirming. Each time my grandmother lifted the comb (with smoke emanating) away from the stove and bought it precariously toward my hair, I would sit as still as possible. There would be a sizzle of hot grease, and the smell of scorched or burned hair as the comb made its way through a section of my kinky hair. There was always a sigh of relief after each section was completed without a burn. Depending on my demeanor, I could make it through this process without any mishaps. However, in the event that some of my hair should somehow attach itself to the comb. I'd be scolded for not holding my head properly. If I yelped in pain as the result of a burn, I was quickly confronted with that I wasn't really burned but it was simply the hot grease melting. After about one hour or more, I would gladly skip away tossing my newfound tresses to the wind. Depending on the weather, it would be about one week before I was Nappy again.

Fortunately for me, my teenage years came during the seventies. This was an era of "Black Power", black people everywhere had a connection to the motherland. Black was beautiful, so except for the occasional blowout to increase the size of my Afro, my hair suffered very little trauma. The next decade was not quite so uneventful. I think it was during this period that I experimented and wore every hairstyle you can imagine.

Let's begin with the curl, which was simple enough if you were able to control the activator. After several skin eruptions and trips to the dermatologist as a result of the oils used to maintain my curl, I soon abandoned that style and was on my way to discover a new look.

This time I wanted something sleek, so this meant getting a perm. There was only one draw back, I was told I couldn't transform from a curl to a perm without serious hair damage, so a trip to the barbershop was imminent. Once again, I emerged with a short Afro. The growth of my hair was not progressing at the rate I'd anticipated, so I decided to wear my hair braided for a while. Throughout the months that followed I toyed with a variety of braided styles. Eventually, my hair reached a desirable length and I was on my way to experience my first chemical perm.

I walked into the salon, toting a magazine in which there was a picture of the style I desired. When I showed the picture to the stylist and expressed my wish to accomplish that same style, she gave me a look as if to say "this is a salon, not a magic shop", but instead she was rather polite, showed me other pictures and suggested that maybe I should pick another style. Not to be deterred, I insisted I wanted the style I had originally chosen. Needless to say, the end result was a total disaster. This was only the beginning of countless frustrating trips to a series of different salons. I soon discovered that in order for me to achieve the look I wanted, I would have to let the perm stay on my hair a little longer. When a stylist would ask me if I was burning I would lie and say no, the whole while wishing I could somehow extinguish the inferno that was consuming my entire head. There was no way I wasn't going to get my hair none straight. Of course that was very foolish of me.

At some point I became tried of the shorter styles, and my motto became "if you can't grow it, buy it". The first weave I wore was sewn in, but I felt it was too bulky and appeared fake, so I graduated to another type of weave. This time I had tracks of hair glued to my scalp. I was ecstatic, at last I had found a style that was flexible and no one knew it was a weave, unless of course you figured out I didn't grow that much hair overnight. It really didn't matter anyway; it was a choice I'd made. The process of removing and replenishing the weave, took a toll of its own. Frequently, the track of hair would be extracted taking with it precious follicles of hair.

It was this cycle and the months of frustration that bought me back to the summer of 1996, and once again a trip to the barbershop. Only this time it was for keeps."

Debbie's Journey

"I call them my children"

"Girl my lociversary is February 18th can you believe it!".

Actually, I couldn't believe almost an entire year had passed since Debbie had made the pledge to lock. Our initial meeting was over the phone. A mutual friend's husband (someone I used to go to church with and hadn't seen in years) connected us. Amazingly, the friend's wife is Debbie's cousin!! Small world huh!

Debbie is part of a sister dynamic duo that owns an art gallery…cleverly titled *II Sisters Art Gallery*. According to Debbie "Lorraine is the organized one"…according to friends and family Debbie is the marketer of the business. At any rate, our initial contact was strictly business. I telephoned her about participating as a vendor at the Nappy & Happy conference I was organizing. Well, once she agreed and business was out of the way… we started talking…I am sure we talked for well over an hour. We had so much in common. I shared with her that there was going to be a gathering of sister-friends to look over some Afro centric clothing Kathy and I were selling. She couldn't wait to attend!

Gloria's house was packed with nappy, "peazy", kinky headed happy women many of whom were locked. We were having a ball, trying on clothes, eating drinking and admiring ourselves. Debbie and Julia came after the fun had started but wasted no time in joining in.

Both cousins were striking Nubian sisters with very close-cropped Afros. Debbie's silver hair glistened in the light. It was beautiful. She started to ask questions about locking. Of course there were so many of us there and all of us were willing to oblige with information she couldn't help but be swayed. She left that evening with at least 4 ethnic outfits and a commitment to start letting her hair grow so she could begin the process of locking.

Over several months we connected, usually at art events at the studio. Each time the conversation would drift toward hair. "I don't know about this…you know I don't like a lot of hair she'd say. "You'll adjust I'd reply …give it time" Or she'd say "My hair isn't growing…it will never get long enough to start…I want your hair!!" I would again give her my support and encourage her to hang with the process…."this is a journey your on, just hang in there".

Finally, this past summer her hair reach a length were it was possible to being her locks (rat-tail comb method). She was ecstatic! When I saw her that first time, floating down the stairs looking all, Nubian queen-like with her Afro centric garb and mini-little twist, to greet her guest at yet another event. She was glowing. "Look!! Look!! At my hair isn't it beautiful!!

"Yeah girl you are looking good!", I said

Debbie struggled with the so-called "ugly stage", never wanting a strand of hair out of place. "No, No way can I let this stuff stay like this (small strands of hair coming out of a twist)…I have got to have my hair done every two weeks. I drive down to Bridgeport after work and have this woman do it".

We talked about how she needed to let her hair get a "grip"… allowing her hair remember how to do the coil thing all on its own. We spoke of how over grooming would weaken the hair and her tiny buds would break off. She still struggled with this idea until going to Bridgeport became a hassle. She opted to have her cousin's husband's loctician groom her hair. "She even comes to the house…but she told me I would have to do it her way (no every two week grooming) or she wouldn't do my hair…and guess what its finally really locking!!"

Recently we spoke on the phone. "You know Sharon I have had my hair natural for over 20 years, I had gone through many phases with it until that point. I am at a different phase now. I could kick my self for not listening about the grooming thing. I would probably be all the way locked by now. Something finally clicked with me. It's not about whether they stick out. It is about me being what I want to be and letting them be. I call them my children and my children or happy. I feel good about the fact that my children are happy and so am I."

Babz's Journey

"You can't save the world…you can't do GOD's work"

I first met Babz at an art gallery open house about a year ago. There she was, standing there with the longest locks I had ever seen. She looked so regal and seemed so spiritual.

One evening over the phone we talked hair and Babz shared her nappy journey. " I am 38 years old and have been natural for 21 of those 38 years. I had perms, weaves, braids, jheri curls you name it. At some point I got tired of being concerned about my hair. You know when you are putting so much energy into worrying about your hair you can't save the world…you can't do God's work!

My relationship with my hair was one of challenge. I never felt great about it. I had to perm it often; it was constantly on my mind. Having processed hair limited me. If I thought my hair was not looking good I didn't go out. I missed some good parties and events because of my hair.

So I decided to cut it all off…I mean a close-cropped razor cut! My mother didn't talk to me for 2 weeks! She couldn't understand why I would do such a thing. I think she thought I was a lesbian…she was afraid that any minute I was going to come out! My mother was not the only person who did not like my new look. Men didn't appreciate it either. Needless to say I just did what I was comfortable with.

Seven years ago I decided to lock my hair. I let it grow in and then did the double –twist method to begin my locks. My mother liked that look; although she was concerned that I wouldn't get married or find a good job with my hair looking like "that". As my locks grew she grew to like them even more. I think the fact that I met my now husband and had a good job helped!

Since I have had locks I have grown spiritually. It is difficult to articulate how or what that is about but it is there. It is about my mind, I can see the whole world. Its liberating, I am becoming the women I always wanted to be…. independent, sexy, smart, not a slave to anyone

The responses I get about my hair are interesting. Many Black people are negative or they'll say the locks look good on me but they could never do that. Others think I must be an artist or something…like I couldn't have my hair looking like this and be a professional. And White people want to touch it! I've had a number of people from the Caribbean say that the way I am wearing my hair is a fad! It's not a fad…I am not going to get tried and cut them off. I think their response has something to do with their culture and the fact that I have cultivated locks. I do think that there are a lot of Black people who appreciate that we are bring locks into the Boardroom and it's ok. Maybe it also has to do with that that there are more people locking. Funny….I see more young brothers locking than young sisters!

When I asked Babz what was the most painful and the most exhilarating thing she could think of related to having natural hair she responded. "Wow! My mother's reaction to my cutting my hair. That was painful. No one can hurt or praise you the way your mother can.

The most exhilarating was just yesterday when my 6 year old daughter said, I love your hair. I want to have my hair in locks like you…I want to be like you. With all the images that surround her in this world, it is the image of her mother that is most important!

Epilogue

All of the journeys that were shared in this book continue. For no journey is truly over until we have left this place. And then...a totally new kind of journey begins. I have loved sharing the smiles, tears, laughter, pain and exhilaration with you. I hope your journey is one of support, love and admiration.

Peace and Blessings,
Sharon

Sources

Part I

Byrd, Ayana and Lori L. Tharps. Hair Story: Untangling The Roots of Black Hair in America. New York: St. Martin's Press, 2001

Evans, Nekhena. Everything You Need to Know About Hairlocking: Dread, African & Nubian Locks. Brooklyn: A&B Publishers Group, 1996

Part II

Bonner, Lonnice Brittenum. Good Hair: For Colored Girls Who've Considered Weaves When The Chemicals Became Too Ruff. New York: Crown Publishers Inc., 1991

Bonner, Lonnice Brittenum. Plaited Glory: For Colored Girls Who've Considered Braids, Locks and Twists. New York: Three Rivers Press, 1996

Kinard, Tulani. No Lye! : The African-American Woman's Guide To Natural Hair Care. New York: St. Martin's Griffin, 1997